Tailwinds across America

Tailwinds

ACROSS AMERICA

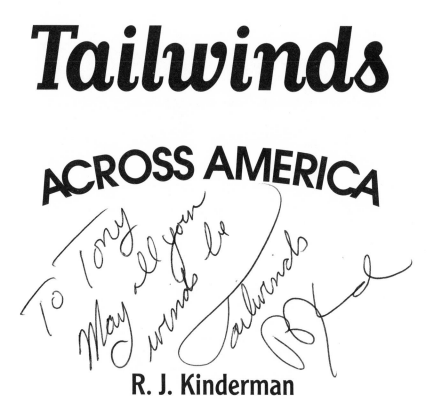

To Tony
May all your
winds be
Tailwinds

R. J. Kinderman

SPINNING WHEELS
PUBLISHING

Interior photos by Denise Kinderman and R.J. Kinderman.

Publisher's Cataloging-in-Publication Data
(Provided by Quality Books, Inc.)

Kinderman, R.J.
  Tailwinds across America / R.J. Kinderman--1st ed.
    p. cm.
    2nd edition, 2015
    ISBN: 978-0-9856469-0-5 --1st ed. Hardcover
    ISBN: 978-0-9856469-3-6 --2nd ed. Softcover
  1. Kinderman, R.J.--Travel--United States 2. Bicycle Touring--United States. 3. United States--Description and travel. I. Title.

GV1044.K562012   796.64
                                QBI12-600117

Printed in the United States of America by McNaughton & Gunn, Inc.

To my parents
Robert and Margaret

He, who inspired a love of adventures,
She, a love to read, and now write, about them.

and
David Myers
Till we meet again

Contents

Acknowledgments

THIS IS A STORY of two adventures. The first took place in 1981, when Denise and I crossed the United States on bicycles. The second began in May 2011, when I first pushed a pen across paper and began writing *Tailwinds across America*. In both cases, I relied heavily on friends and strangers. I am particularly grateful to the following people, without whose assistance I would have never overcome the mountains and headwinds of writing and publishing:

Penny Swan, my friend for over 20 years, who converted eight legal pads of scrawl into a neat, legible manuscript. Her patience and support were invaluable.

Marian Wolden and Michael Ubbelohde, two high school language arts teachers, may have found making corrections to student grammar a piece of cake compared to aiding in the first edit for a retired principal.

Richard Rubesch and Hugh Miller, with the patience of Job, guided me through and often saved me from the terrors of technology.

Dennis Weidemann, author and my unofficial mentor, like people met along our trip, gave help to a complete stranger. Linda Weidemann, with the eyes of an artist, created from parts a beautiful book. Heather McElwain, final editor, gently brought me through a revision process with guidance and patience, and helped me understand how to bring memories to life. Special thanks to Sue Boshers and her eagle eye while proofreading.

To all the friends and strangers who appear in *Tailwinds across America*: Without all of you, neither of these two adventures would have happened.

And, most importantly,
To Denise
My partner on the road and in life.
My tailwind.

There's a race of men who don't fit in,
A race that can't stay still;
So they break the hearts of kith and kin,
And they roam the world at will.
They range the field and rove the flood,
And climb the mountain's crest;
For theirs is the curse of the gypsy blood,
And for them there is no rest.

—Robert W. Service, from "The Men That Don't Fit In,"
published in *The Spell of the Yukon and Other Verses,* 1907

Preface

CRESTING LOGAN PASS on the "Going-to-the-Sun" Road in Glacier National Park, I flew down the mountain as wind blasted my face. Seconds earlier, I had blown past a melting snowbank, leaving the rims on my bicycle wet and, for the moment, my brakes useless. Approaching a pickup truck, I had no choice but to pass him on the left and, as I zipped by, the driver yelled out his speed—"42 miles an hour!"

Pulling in front of him, I certainly felt fear, but it had been seasoned with exhilaration. This wasn't how I had planned this descent. Winding down the mountain at breakneck speed, I rode that fine edge where caution would have been the prudent response. Even once my rims had dried off and my brakes again functioned, I chose to let the thrill and adrenaline override prudence as I accelerated down the mountain.

We were two weeks into a bike ride across America, which certainly turned out to be one heck of a ride, and in that moment I understood, in a very literal sense, where the phrase "throwing caution to the wind" came from. I realized that sometimes we just have to let off the brakes, let the wind slap our face, and enjoy the ride.

IN 1981, MY friend Denise Egge and I loaded our bikes on a Northwest Airlines flight, threw caution to the wind, and began chasing a dream with a few hundred bucks in our pockets. As I prepared for this trip I was frequently asked, "How can you afford to take off the summer and not earn some money for school?" My answer was always the same, "How can I afford not to?" I've made my share of wrong decisions in my life, but in 1981, I thank God that I got that one right. Life is a gift, and I knew then that it was important to live it to the fullest.

WHAT I DIDN'T know at that time was that years later, as I juggled a very busy personal and professional life, I would lose touch with what had been so important to me in 1981.

On July 3, 2001, I received a diagnosis of colon cancer. For a time, I worried about my future or if I even had one. Following surgery and an ongoing physical recovery, I found myself in an emotional hell from which I felt unable to escape. When a deep depression pulled me down, a friend visited and brought me a copy of Lance Armstrong's book, *It's Not about the Bike,* a powerful recounting of his journey back to life after cancer. Despite odds stacked against him, Lance overcame his diagnosis. His book got my wheels rolling again, moving me forward, and most importantly, reminded me of how I had embraced life when Denise and I biked across America in 1981.

People say everything happens for a reason. Although I would have preferred to skip the cancer battle, the experience reminded me that life—just like our bike trip—was about the journey, not the destination. Remembering those days Denise and I spent on the road helped me find my way back to a much fuller, rewarding life. And just as Lance Armstrong's book was "not about the bike," *Tailwinds across America* is about much more than just the miles covered. On our incredible cross-country bike journey, just as in life, we crossed paths with some of the kindest people I've ever met, as well as some who literally tried to run us over. We cranked our bikes up tortuous mountain climbs, but also coasted almost surreally beautiful descents that stretched for miles and miles. We experienced the downside of development in the name of progress, but we were also treated to beauty that can only be attributed to the bounty of nature. We faced days of unrelenting headwinds that had the capacity to drain our desire to continue, but these were eclipsed by the days when the sun was in my face, my friend was by my side, and God's gift to all cyclists—tailwinds—were at our back.

This was not a story to be written in 1981. Although an incredible experience at that time, the story then would have lacked the enhancement that can only be delivered by 30 years of life and reflection. I worked from the daily journals that I had painstakingly recorded, despite sometimes indescribable bone and butt weariness from long days in the saddle. At times, I found it unbelievable that Denise and I had made this journey. The physical challenges had been substantial, but even more so were the circumstances and conventional wisdoms that worked to keep us "in the box."

To all those with your own dreams, whether from your past or for the future, realized or still a work in progress, I invite you along on this ride. Perhaps it will propel you forward as you catch your own tailwinds.

Tailwinds across America

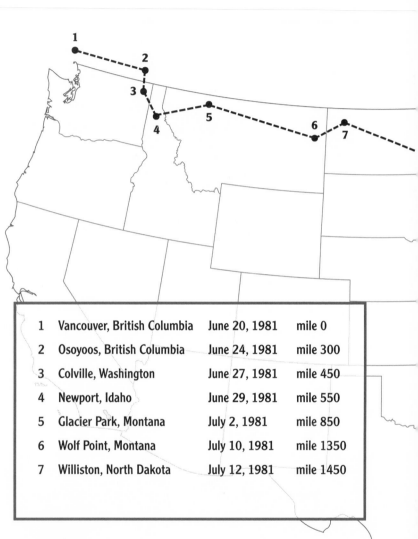

1	Vancouver, British Columbia	June 20, 1981	mile 0
2	Osoyoos, British Columbia	June 24, 1981	mile 300
3	Colville, Washington	June 27, 1981	mile 450
4	Newport, Idaho	June 29, 1981	mile 550
5	Glacier Park, Montana	July 2, 1981	mile 850
6	Wolf Point, Montana	July 10, 1981	mile 1350
7	Williston, North Dakota	July 12, 1981	mile 1450

8	Minneapolis, Minnesota	July 19, 1981	mile 1970
9	Oshkosh, Wisconsin	July 23, 1981	mile 2400
10	Ludington, Michigan	July 27, 1981	mile 2500
11	Simcoe, Ontario	August 1, 1981	mile 2925
12	Pultneyville, New York	August 3, 1981	mile 3150
13	Springfield, Vermont	August 6, 1981	mile 3475
14	Rochester, New Hampshire	August 7, 1981	mile 3590
15	Owls Head, Maine	August 8, 1981	mile 3725

CHAPTER 1

Inspired to Dream

LOOKING DOWN from 30,000 feet in the sky, I saw an illusion of serenity—not good, not bad, but more like a watercolor painting in which the sharp edges had been blurred. From this perspective, we gave no forethought to steep climbs or long downhills or to impatient, hand-on-the-horn, get-off-my-road drivers. And we certainly did not anticipate meeting families who would open their homes to strangers. We did not feel the hot or cold, the wet or dry, the misery of headwinds nor the joy of tailwinds. From the plane, everything appeared neat, tidy, and organized; below, we saw the live version of the maps we'd poured over in the earliest stages of our "what if" dreams.

The difference with this day—June 20, 1981—was that this dream was moving forward. I grew up a blue-collar kid, the son of a man who told stories of growing up in the Depression, working in the Civilian Conservation Corps, enlisting in the Navy, and becoming a Pearl Harbor survivor. My father sailed with Halsey's fleet in the South Pacific, along the way surviving frontline action and being sunk in a typhoon in 1944. I could never get enough of his stories of a life on the edge, and I recognized that although my father abhorred the war, he lived for adventure. He trudged through a 30-year career as a factory machinist, doing his best to make a good life for our family, but he was "born for the storm," and as a child, I lived for time spent with him on the water or in the woods. His stories of hitchhiking across the country, working in the northern Wisconsin forests, and a host of other adventures planted a seed in my soul. On that plane to begin my own adventure, this seed bore fruit, not for the first time, nor for the last.

I HAD MET my friend and trip partner Denise in the fall of 1980, on the track at UW–River Falls, Wisconsin. She had already graduated from college with a degree in physical education, and was employed as the resident manager at a halfway house for teens going through drug rehab. A daughter of the Iron Range in Virginia, Minnesota, she was part of a tough group of people who knew about hard work. On our trip, I experienced time and again that she was no exception. She gave up her job, sold her Pontiac Firebird, purchased a new Wisconsin-made Trek ten-speed, and never looked back.

This trip was born on the heels of another. In August 1980, Steve Katner, a college friend, felt his own need for "one last fling," so to speak. He had recently graduated, and although he appreciated the benefits of gainful employment, he found corporate life extracted a certain part of his soul, or certainly most of his time. To combat this, Steve had a great idea that he and I should bike from Tallahassee, Florida, on the Gulf Coast, back to northern Wisconsin. For the two of us, in our mid-20s and in the best shape of our lives, it was grueling. I will leave it to your imagination to picture a 1,600-mile bike trip from Florida in the middle of August with a maximum of 16 days from start to finish (Steve only had two weeks off from his new job). This dream included riding in temperatures of 110 degrees Fahrenheit, averaging 115 miles a day, and sleeping in places our mothers wouldn't approve of.

Despite the physical challenges of our Florida trip, we thrived on our adventure, and after a very short period of time following the trip, I found a new set of maps beckoning me.

"IGNORANCE IS BLISS" is often the foundation of many great endeavors of youthfulness, yet there are definitely advantages to both sides of the coin of age. "What if?" is the flip side question of experience, and although it undoubtedly can save us from many mishaps, it can also deprive us of many rewarding experiences. As Denise and I prepared for our trip across America, we heard plenty from both sides. This is not to say anyone tried to talk us out of our plans, but we heard many variations of the potential doom awaiting. People didn't say, "You'll be hit by a truck and killed." Instead, they asked, "Do you have any idea of how many cars and trucks will pass within inches of you?" Or, "Do you know what will happen if your brakes go out coming down a mountain full speed?" Fortunately for us, we heard much more of "Man, I'd give anything to do that," or "Biking in the mountains will be incredible." Like most people with their minds made up, Denise and I banked the positive feedback and rationalized the negative possibilities as overcautiousness.

Northern Wisconsin is not the dream environment for most cyclists. For us, it meant enduring most of our training rides in weather best suited to ducks and penguins. On one April ride frozen into my memory, rain turned to sleet that turned to snow. As if this were not enough, someone stole all our money from a bike pack; our meals for the next two days revolved around a loaf of bread and water bottles.

As spring came into bloom, we did as well. By the time we reached our departure date in June, we had logged over 1,500 miles of riding, no small feat in the northern tier of states. Our bodies adjusted as we put in the miles and shed the pounds. We needed to be mechanically self-sufficient on our journey; thus part of our training involved attaining proficiency in dealing with flat tires, broken spokes, and derailleur adjustments—all of which had improved to a fair level of competence.

We knew we would also be limited in the gear we could carry (approximately 28 pounds each), so like kids at Christmas, we made our lists and checked them twice…and three times, until we had limited everything to essentials. Ours was *not* a trip akin to a group booking with Bike Across America. We would have no sag wagons, limited restaurant stops, few motels, and certainly no accompanying massage therapists. This was way before everyone was connected via cell phone, neither of us had a credit card to bail us out, should we need it, and an ATM didn't exist. What we did have was a small backpack stove, tent, sleeping bags, a few clothes, and a combined total of $475.00 to cover everything for about 60 days, or about $4.00 a day each. We also had a much-appreciated book of McDonald's gift certificates from my sister, Mary, and we planned to stash as many packets of the in-flight peanuts in our pockets as we could.

With the help of my parents, we stored our limited possessions for the summer and canceled our apartment leases. At the airport, we said good-bye to my folks. My dad gave a look that said, "I don't know if this is a good idea, but go for it because I wish I could go." My mom looked a little more like she was sending me to fight in Vietnam rather than to bike across the country. Both were supporters, however, and with the usual extended Wisconsin good-bye, we were finally off, or at least awaiting takeoff.

At that time, no one in airport security batted an eye at packed knives, fuel bottles, or matches. Our main concern was that our bikes and gear would arrive at the same place we did. Our panniers were packed and strapped, and our bikes dismantled and in boxes. Needless to say, we did not fly first class, but rather back in herd class where the cramped seating prepared us for 60 days in a tiny tent. As budget travelers, we booked the cheapest flight possible. Only through the eyes of youth were we able to think that flying from Minneapolis to Duluth, Duluth to Winnipeg, Winnipeg to Calgary, and Calgary to Vancouver would be a great way to see more of the country.

As we leveled off at 30,000 feet, Denise looked at me and asked, "Do you think we forgot anything?" I couldn't imagine what, but I responded, "I'm sure of it." Looking out my window at the Cascade Mountains stacked in a seemingly relentless row upon row of precipitous peaks, I questioned if perhaps I'd forgotten my sanity.

AT 5:30 P.M. Pacific time on that first day, we touched down in Vancouver Island, British Columbia. Leaving the jet, we were concerned about our bikes and gear. With all the transfers on our hopscotch across the continent, we had our fingers crossed.

We shared a sigh of relief when *almost* all of our things arrived. The worst that had happened was that a baggage handler had taken some four-leaf clover pins off my packs. A friend had given me the pins before the trip from Florida to Wisconsin, and they had meant a lot to me—offering good luck through some tough situations. The loss was tempered, though, by amusement with an addition to a kangaroo illustration I had on my bike box: Someone (maybe that same baggage handler) had drawn piles of poop under it. If stealing pins and drawing poop on my bike box was some baggage handler's version of throwing caution to the wind, I was happy to donate the pins: I figured that guy needed all of the luck he could get.

CHAPTER 2

Rain, Slugs, and Landslides

TEARING OPEN our bike boxes and breaking out our tools, we staked out a spot in the baggage claim area. As waves of people rushed by, we posed enough of an oddity to draw the attention of numerous travelers. While creating bicycles from a pile of wheels, frames, handlebars, and seat posts, we drew the first of many inquiries as to our intentions: "Where ya going?" "Whatcha doing?" People fell into one of two camps, with responses of either "Are you nuts?" or "Man, I wish I could do something like that." However, in almost all cases, even those who thought we were crazy also gave us looks of envy. I wouldn't say they all wanted to bike 4,000 miles, but they did equate the trip with a dream of breaking out from some grind or rut into which many of us slip. Throughout the summer, we met hundreds of people who opened their lives and homes to us. Although *we* were grateful recipients of their kindness, we often found that time and again, they would thank *us*. In sharing our dreams with them, they themselves found a brief respite from their life's challenges.

We took turns hitting the restroom at the air terminal to change into our biking clothes. As I emerged from the bathroom, it was hardly with the confident transformation of Superman leaving the phone booth. We were not yet familiar with spandex and after a few days on the road in the rain, our wool shorts were anything but formfitting.

AT 7:00 P.M. we were still in the airport terminal in a city of over a million people—and oh yeah, on an island. We had three possible ways off the island: by boat (not an option), by bridge (no bikes allowed after 5:00 P.M.), or by tunnel, which was the only legal route for bikes at this time of night.

With our pile of parts now transformed into road-ready bicycles, we strapped on our panniers and rolled out into the crowds of people. Wheeling up to a car rental booth, I asked the attendant, "What do you think about biking through the tunnel?" The look on his face was as if I had asked, "How about if we camped in a rifle range?" In a very concerned tone, he indicated that the tunnel would be suicide; he explained that if we didn't get hit, we would probably be overcome by exhaust fumes. "What about the bridge?" I asked. He thought for a second, and responded, "That would be illegal, but I'd rather be illegal and alive than legal and dead!"

Good enough for us, and with that, our adventure truly began. Every journey starts with that first step, or, in this case, a push of the pedal. So, out the doors of the terminal we went, forging into the overcast and raining weather as thousands of cars passed within inches of our handlebars.

That first day and night of any such trip can be the most difficult, and this was no exception. We were tired, wet, didn't know a soul, and yes, lost. It couldn't get worse, I thought. But as I tried to lead us out of the current quagmire, I heard a POW! Thoughts whirled through my mind. Gunshot? Firecracker? Denise, riding just behind me, knew instantly that she had blown a front tire. As we ground to a stop, it was easy to see this would be no simple flat. The front tire was slashed almost completely across and, of course, the tube was destroyed. Neither of us had seen the bottom part of a beer bottle—which only by good luck, I had missed, and only by bad luck, Denise ran squarely over.

Now, Denise was as tough as a boiled owl, but it wasn't hard for me to see that we both needed to put this long first day behind us. Our dilemma, however, was the tire. With fresh new tires and tubes, we expected the tires to last for over a thousand miles, so we had packed only spare tubes. This tire slash ran across the entire face of the tire, with only the bead intact. Although the new tube worked great, it protruded through the slash. As rain dripped off my nose and passing traffic kept up a steady splash, I scanned in all directions for a possible bike or sporting goods shop. Fat chance of that!

I felt in my bones that the time was upon us to either be doers or dreamers. If we didn't work this out, it was doubtful we would stand up to the many challenges ahead. As I wiped the rain from my eyes to check if a sag wagon was pulling up (hallucination), Denise hit on a brainstorm, an epiphany— duct tape! That's right, that great gray tape that has bailed out countless people from countless messes came to our rescue. Having frequently used duct tape to patch together a whitewater kayak in past adventures, I knew to pack a small spool. We replaced the tube and partially inflated it. We then wrapped the tape over the tire and around the rim about six times. The tape held tighter than a frog's butt and with all the rain we needed something watertight. We were now able to inflate the tube sufficiently to ride on it. The tape, however, would not clear through the brake pads. Simple solution: Open the front brakes and use only the back. With this first major obstacle overcome, we felt as good as two people could for being up 20 hours, flying cross-country, and being lost in the rain on two wheels on a four-lane highway in a major city where each spoken sentence ended with "eh"!

I think we both realized that the success of this trip would lie in our ability to compensate and adjust. I recognized that this would probably be the number one necessity on a trip such as ours. Planning was important, but flexibility would be essential: Roads did not always go where maps said they would, weather predictions were a crapshoot at best, and despite best intentions, mileage goals would be elusive. Multiple times daily, we would need to make adjustments and keep on rolling. A trip of this nature will tell you a lot about yourself and your partner. More than one adventure has met an early demise when partners were unable or unwilling to adjust and do so in a way that did not spur blame, guilt, or a bad attitude. I'm not saying we never had a bad day, but we knew we would need to carry each other through those, even if one of us was sure the other was wrong.

Though our money was limited, we knew that it was a crucial night to get out of the rain, organize our gear, and get a good night's rest. With that, we slogged forward for seven more miles with the steady thump, thump, thump of Denise's tire until we found a cheap, seedy, but for us that night, "home sweet home" motel. Quite a start to our journey! We had faced a lot of issues but undoubtedly more lay ahead of us. Although we knew that hot showers and warm, dry beds would be few and far between, right then we felt good. We had 11 miles down, and only 3,989 miles to go.

"HOW'S THE weather look?" Denise asked the next morning. As I reached to part the curtains, I hoped we had somehow earned a bluebird day with bright sun, light traffic, and the wind at our back. Peering through the rain-streaked window, I was greeted by a sky of gray, heavy clouds and a McDonald's wrapper blowing by.

"It doesn't look too bad," I replied, trying to stay positive. "And I think we can use some of our McDonald's gift certificates for breakfast."

Taking advantage of the hot shower and dry room, we organized our gear, located a bike shop 15 miles down the road, donned our dry clothes and rain gear, and hit the road. Sure enough, in a couple of miles, we treated ourselves to a McDonald's breakfast. As we journeyed eastward, we realized that it was fairly predictable what fast food places we were approaching just by looking in the ditch. Fifteen miles of thump-thumping later, we replaced Denise's front tire, bought a spare, and were back on the road.

WITH A GOOD night's sleep, dry clothes, repairs made, and 20 ounces of McCaffeine in the bloodstream, we were ready to roll. Getting off the Queen's Highway 1 was our first priority. Leaving the majority of traffic in our dust (or more like spray), we jumped on Highway 7A to 7, and followed a broad river valley eastward, headed for Mission. Despite the soggy day, we were happy to be underway. That first—always tough—day was history, and we believed the bad weather couldn't hold forever.

We slogged past midday before taking the opportunity to pull into a park area along the river. It was our good fortune to meet up with three lifeguards who not only invited us in for hot chocolate and a sandwich, but also filled us in on vital information. Lifeguard Bert let us in on a little secret: "It's kind of wet out today, eh?" Shaking a large drop of water off the end of my nose and squeezing a pint of water out of my bike shorts, I gave him my best upbeat Wisconsinite: "Not really too bad at all!"

Lifeguard Will seemed obliged to try to lift our spirits with, "Yeah, it's rained all or part of every day now for the last 57 days." I certainly wasn't about to doubt Will, as we were just approaching 24 straight hours of rain, and it was obvious from the surrounding landscape that this had been happening for some time now. These guys had careers as TV weathermen in their futures, no doubt! As we finished our break, Joe (Lifeguard #3) gave us each a lifeguard T-shirt and joked, "You'll probably need them if the rain keeps up, eh?"

Despite the rain, we were treated to beautiful countryside that day. Everything was certainly green and lush, and banks of fog hung in the valley air. Peddling into Mission, British Columbia, that afternoon, the rain continued and we elected to set up our tent in a roadside stop shared with some Canadian bicyclists. We'd knocked off a 45-mile day, and combined with yesterday's 11 to 12 miles, we were satisfied with our mileage, considering conditions. Denise got to work on our tent as I broke out the stove and fired up some macaroni and cheese. I also bought some pierogies stuffed with a salmon filling from a nearby vendor stand. A simple meal never tasted so good, even if hastily prepared and eaten. Inside the tent, we pulled on dry clothes; this combined with a hot meal gave us that feeling that only comes when you are snug in a tent as the rain drums on the outside of the rain fly. Perhaps not a perfect start to the trip, and in some ways far from it, but we were none the worse for wear. Completing my second day of journal entries I saw Denise was sound asleep. I knew with certainty that there was no place else I'd rather be. Like many 20-somethings, I didn't know for sure what the future held for me but I sensed that I would carry this experience with me the rest of my life.

I DIDN'T NEED a weather report the next morning to know how our day would shape up. The Pacific Northwest was certainly living up to its rainy reputation. I think perhaps the second toughest thing to do on such days is to leave a warm, dry sleeping bag. I say second because the toughest thing is pulling on the same cold, clammy clothes worn the day before. Without bothering with a rain-soaked breakfast, we decided to hit the road and eat during our first break. As I stepped out of the tent, my foot shot out from under me. I landed on my already-wet butt onto saturated ground. As I pushed myself up and reached around to brush off water and dirt from my shorts, my hand met the grossest slime imaginable, and what looked like parts of a snail. As I processed the scene, I spotted a number of huge snails on the ground around me. Inside the tent, Denise had heard my loud "Yuck, what the **** is this **** all over me." She came out to investigate and evidently found humor in the situation, informing me, "Whatever that *is* crushed on the back of your shorts, it has feelers sticking out of it."

Thirty years later, I retrieved a plethora of information about these disgusting things online. They were actually called "black slugs," which leads me to wonder what creative biologist named these babies. They can grow up to six inches in length, of which I was then wearing about four, and they leave a thick trail of slime in their wake as they move about, including up the side of our tent.

At the time, I resorted to cleaning myself with the time-honored method of wiping my hands across my shorts, over and over. I succeeded in spreading a few inches of slime, guts, and parts from the invertebrate over a much larger area of my now-drenched, drooping bike shorts. I suppose that when in Rome you have to live with Romans, but at least the snails in Wisconsin had the decency to live in a shell and stay out of sight for the most part, and they came nowhere near the size of these beasts straight from the film, *Land of the Giants*.

As we packed up our soaked gear, I wondered when we would get a break from the weather. The relentless rain permeated more than just my clothing. It started with the continuous splash of passing cars, spray from my own front wheel, and water streaming into my eyes. This, combined with a metronomic squishing sound of water in my shoes with every revolution of the pedals—80 times a minute, 4,800 times an hour—it dampened my spirit as well. A break in this weather would not come too soon.

The previous night, we had decided we would remain in Canada for a while rather than drop south into the United States. We were discovering that the majority of roads in the Northwest tend to head north and south because the populated areas, such as Vancouver, Victoria, Seattle, and Portland, are stacked north and south. Far fewer roads track directly east and west, and those that do are more circuitous. A person may have to travel a road 100 miles to cover 50 miles as the crow flies. Many times in the week ahead I wished we were crows, but, lacking wings, we decided to continue on Highway 7, shooting for the town of Hope, British Columbia, approximately 55 miles northeast. We hoped this would give us a chance to cross a mountain range and, with luck, leave behind some rain.

As we soldiered on through the rain, I couldn't help but obsess about my slippery bike seat. Although I cannot prove it, I have come to believe slug slime has a viscosity far superior to the highest-grade motor oil. A fortune waits the person who figures out a way to harvest, process, and market the gooey slime.

Nearing Hope, an unbelievably beautiful view emerged from the mist ahead of us. On the previous bike trip from Florida, we had rolled along miles of significant foothills prior to approaching the Smoky Mountains. Here in British Columbia, we had been biking on a table-flat terrain for two days, when the Cascade Mountains erupted out of the fog in front of us. Due to all the moisture, the Cascades were covered in lush green growth. They jutted out of the flatland, reaching into the clouds that seemed stacked up against them. Beautiful as they were, I couldn't help but wonder what type of road and elevation gains awaited us. In the interests of "ignorance is bliss," we found comfort in not knowing.

Wet, hungry, and tired, we pulled into Hope and stopped at a small store to buy sandwich meat, bread, and a quart of milk. We found a laundromat, perched our waterlogged butts on benches usually reserved for folding clothes, ate lunch, and took the opportunity to dry wet clothes. Surrounded by stacks of people's unmentionables, engulfed by the aroma of detergent, and serenaded by the thumping of dryers, we enjoyed dining at its finest.

Our sophisticated appearance drew the attention of another laundromat patron by the name of Peter, a helicopter pilot from Australia working various contract jobs in the area. He invited us to stop by his friend Maggie's house. During this brief visit, Pete told us that, "If you're planning on heading east tomorrow, you're going to have a tough slog, mate." He explained that 15 years ago, half of the mountain slid down and covered the road for miles. Known as the Hope Slide, it was the largest landslide ever recorded in Canada, and had claimed the lives of several people when it occurred. Crews had been working to restore the roadway for over 10 years and although a passage through was open, 10 to 15 miles were still rough and unpaved. In addition, we learned that we would need to be through the area by 10:00 A.M., after which a crew closed the passage to dynamite the mountain of rock still blocking the way.

Pete and Maggie suggested a campground a short distance down the road, and we decided that the hot showers the site offered were worth the few extra miles. As we set up camp, we noticed a small, very low tent set up relatively nearby. We never did see who, or for that matter, what, was staying in it; strange grunting noises continued to emanate from the tent—and trust me, I don't think love was in the air—accompanied by movement within that caused the tent to pop outward on the sides. Animal or human, we never did determine. Either way, it freaked us out and we elected to skip a Welcome Wagon visit with our mysterious neighbors as they bumped and grunted the night away.

IT WAS NOW June 23, and I couldn't believe the rain had not stopped for one minute since we left the airport four days ago. We got an early start at 6:30 A.M., to avoid getting dynamited, and found ourselves hitting some significant climbs. As we approached the area of the landslide, the roadway narrowed, the pavement disappeared, and we found ourselves in a much more cozy relationship with cars and trucks. The good news was that we had a shoulder to ride on. The bad news was that the entire roadway was like an unpaved shoulder. We're talking wet, soupy mud littered with a fair number of golf ball– to softball-sized rocks more suited to mountain bikes than our narrow-tired ten-speeds made for paved roads. As hard as we tried to maintain momentum, riding uphill in sloppy mud caused us to regularly lose balance and start again. We managed to absorb much of the splatter from passing vehicles, and found ourselves covered in mud from head to toe in no time at all. Appearances aside, we soon encountered a more significant problem: Our derailleurs stopped functioning because of all of the mud caking them. The upside of this was that we frequently got to stretch our legs and give our butts a rest because the only way we were going forward was by walking or jogging our bikes. We improvised a fix by squirting water from our water bottles on the derailleurs. This cleaned them enough to somewhat function. At one point, we even dipped our bikes in a stream that bordered the roadway.

Nearing the actual roadwork area, traffic became stop and go (for the cars, as well as us). After ten long, arduous, sloppy, miserable miles, we cleared the last of the work crews and were back on pavement. With one final bike dip in a stream, we continued our climb. Now free of mud, we found that biking in the rain on pavement actually felt like a gift.

This day had been a push to be sure—with the early start, rain, mud, and the construction work. But we had actually climbed 47 miles and upon cresting Hope Pass emerged into clear skies and wonderful sunshine. This, in and of itself, should have been more than we could have expected, but the cake was frosted with almost 40 miles of a splatter-free sunny downhill ride. At 35 miles an hour, we felt incredible elation that the gravity that had tortured us for countless hours was now pulling us effortlessly into a sun-filled valley. We rolled to the end of an 86-mile day and set up camp along a scenic river just outside of Princeton, British Columbia. That night, we shared our campsite with three other bikers, two women at the front end of a trip eastward across Canada and a solo guy only three days out from finishing his trip from east to west. Tired, but very happy, we celebrated with a dinner of chunky chicken soup and hot chocolate. Shadows—unseen during the previous days of rain—slid over us as the sun set behind us.

DESPITE COOL EVENING temperatures, sunshine warmed our tent as we rose. What a simple joy to start a day dry and warm. The previous night, one of our campmates explained that we were heading into a drier desertlike environment now that we were on the eastern side of the Cascade Mountains.

I attempted to break the news gently to him that he could expect somewhat different road and moisture conditions as he reversed our track. I hoped things would change for him because it would be a miserable way to finish a cross-country trip.

Inhaling a hearty breakfast of mac and cheese, we tore into our bikes, stripping them down, cleaning chains and derailleurs, and I replaced a tube that had been slowly leaking. With an attitude far improved from 24 hours earlier, we mounted up wearing only T-shirts and shorts, and headed out Highway 3 toward Osoyoos, British Columbia. For the first 13 miles, we enjoyed a gentle downhill. However, we soon had to pay the piper as we began a 14-mile climb up to Richter Pass. With nice weather and a good road, it seemed like a ride in the park.

CHAPTER 3

Gypsies, Rainbows, and Desperados

AFTER THREE DAYS of nothing but rain, 72 miles of pure sunshine left us feeling fried, living proof of the old adage about too much of a good thing. Rolling into Osoyoos, British Columbia, it seemed like the Bing cherry capital of the world, as they celebrated the Cherry Festival. Walking our bikes through town, hundreds of people on the street moved along in that bump-and-go sort of way one travels in a crowd. Waiting to cross a street, I watched a man attempt to pick a wallet from another man's pocket. Luckily, he missed, but when I mentioned this to someone, he laughed and shrugged it off, saying, "Ha! The gypsies." I looked at him in disbelief, and he explained that cherry harvest (and festival) time brought hundreds of gypsies to the area for work, as well as to practice their other skills. With a very limited amount of resources for our trip, we moved our funds to under our clothing and made certain not to leave our bikes and gear unattended.

While we made plans on a corner, an elderly gentleman came up to us and inquired about our trip details. I explained where we were from, where we started, and where we were headed as the old man just shook his head in amazement. Shaking my hand he said, "I think it's just great you are taking the time to do this with your son." He looked so pleased that I didn't have it in me to correct him. I don't know which of us took it harder, me being only 18 months older than Denise, or her, who certainly was not my son.

With all the activity in town and not wanting to stand guard over our gear (I mean, gypsies, really! I thought they were made for TV), we decided to head to the countryside to camp. The cheapest campground was $6.50 a night, and our finances were already pretty taxed so we opted for creativity. Heading out of town, we saw a beautiful lake surrounded by mountains. Above the lake, a farmer was working in a hillside orchard with thousands of cherry trees. We pedaled to him, introduced ourselves, and explained our situation. After we assured him we would make no mess, he gave us permission to camp, showing us a grassy site on a hill.

Looking out the end of our tent, I saw thousands of fruit-laden cherry trees ringing a beautiful lake with mountains in the background—all softened by a setting sun. I thanked God for this time, and realized we were only a short way into our journey. Before the first spin of the pedals on this trip I had anticipated a plethora of new encounters. Only a few days into our journey I could hardly believe what we had already experienced in such a short time—the airport, rain, mountains, slugs, gypsies—and I wouldn't have traded any of it. These were the reasons I knew I had to make this trip.

We had planned to drop back into the United States the next day, and not cross into Canada again until we reached Michigan and headed into Ontario. That would be many miles away though, and with that thought, I popped one last Bing cherry into my mouth, dumped a way-too-large pile of pits out the door, and drifted off to sleep.

WITH A BEAUTIFUL morning beckoning and a breakfast of perfect cherries fresh off the trees, we bid good-bye to our perfect campsite. By this point in our trip, Canada had certainly saved its best for last, and as we contemplated leaving, we felt grateful for the hospitality given us. I thought about how different two countries could seem in some regards, yet similar in so many others. The Canadian scenery was breathtaking, and the people, friendly and helpful. For anyone who has traveled in a similar manner, you know the importance of receiving kindness from strangers. It seemed people opened their homes and lives in a manner that they probably never would have had we been on motorcycles or in cars. I wondered if this had something to do with a perceived vulnerability that made us appear less threatening and more trustworthy.

Breaking camp, Denise had a good suggestion: "What do you think about mailing back some of our cold-weather gear?" We debated back and forth, guessing whether or not we would encounter more cold weather. If we had been traveling in a car, we would not have even had this conversation, but when carrying every pound on a bike, we looked to economize. We soon decided to ship a small pile of gear, including one item as a treat for when we finished.

Throughout the miles and miles we had biked this past week, we had found it impossible to keep ahead on calories. Anything tasted good when that hungry, but a favorite treat was one we discovered in Canada: fruit leather. The first time we tried the sheets of various dried and pressed fruits, we fell in love with the taste and found it provided great energy. We hadn't seen this in the states at that time, so we thought a pound of it awaiting us at the end would be pretty sweet. In all, we shipped home about six pounds of gear, and although it doesn't sound like a lot, it made a difference.

Crossing into the United States on Highway 97, we headed due south for the first time. We joked that if we had broken any laws in Canada, the Royal Canadian Mounted Police would have no difficulty tracking us down: All they would have had to do was follow the trail of cherry pits down the highway as we ate from our front packs. We were like Hansel and Gretel with cherry pits.

THOUGH WE TRIED not to be slaves to our maps, we always focused our attention eastward. We were now truly in a desert environment on the east side of the Cascades, drenched in sunshine. It was hard to believe the rain and cold we had traveled through.

With a flat road and 90-degree temperatures in the far northern part of Washington, we rolled along until we hit Highway 20 and were once again eastward bound and climbing. Along the way, we encountered a few people, but they didn't appear to be typical travelers. Not that we fit the bill of typical either, but these folks had an "earthy" look to them. The first group went by in an old pickup. A bit later, we came upon another group, maybe a family, in a wagon pulled by mules. They sort of looked like the gypsies, only not as colorful. As we took a break at a rest area, a tall cowboy-looking guy (hat, boots, shirt, the works) approached us.

"Where you folks heading?" he drawled. We introduced ourselves and gave him the quick-version itinerary. Upon hearing this, he looked a little relieved and said, "For a minute there I thought you were more of those 'Rainbow people' we got flooding the area." It turned out that the folks we were seeing were all heading to their annual "Rainbow Gathering." As best I can describe them, the Rainbow people were kind of leftover hippies from the 1960s. Each year they converged on an area for their version of the Mountain Man Rendezvous. The Rainbow people's clothes were a bit different, as was their music, and although mountain men smoked pipes, I think these folks were blowing a different smoke.

Our newfound cowboy buddy introduced himself as "Tex Sword, worm farmer." He gave me one of his business cards featuring a night crawler wearing a cowboy hat and bandanna and twirling a lariat. Tex was a nice guy, and he didn't dislike the Rainbow people, though they were a bit "out there" for a worm rancher. He shared an experience of an encounter with them the previous year. He described their gathering/camp area just up the road near a town called Newport. As a member of the volunteer fire department, Tex and his crew had been called to the campsite. (They had arrived to Rainbow people numbering in the thousands.) Tex went on to explain, "We pulled up the truck and we couldn't believe our eyes. There they were, Rainbow people smoking dope; men, women, and children running around half naked, singing, dancing. It was a sight."

"Was the fire a big one?" I asked.

As Tex looked at the mule team family that was coming up behind us, he just wagged his head and replied, "Hell, I don't know. We just turned around and went home!"

With a tip of the hat to Tex, we started thinking about a place to camp for the night.

TRAVELING BY BIKE placed us in situations we would not have experienced by car, train, or plane. Senses were tuned in to the myriad of sounds and sensations absent when enclosed in a vehicle. We felt firsthand the variations of temperature, and even the various microclimates as we pedaled past snowbanks in the mountains. In the desert environment, waves of heat rose up off the blacktop road. Surrounded by the sounds and scents of nature, we experienced the freshness of morning one moment and were assaulted by not-so-pleasant odors, such as roadkill, the next.

As any cyclist will attest, it is not a good idea to place too much stock in directions or advice from motor travelers. Usually well intended, they lacked the perspective or experience of bicycle travel. Many times I asked a motorist, "How is the road ahead? Are there many hills?" Most of the time I received a response of "Great road, flat as a pancake." But, to an average motorist, a one-mile distance with a 6 percent slope translates to an imperceptible increase in pressure on the gas pedal and a slight increase in fuel consumption. To bicyclists, a 6 percent slope means dropping gears, pushing harder, and bearing down. I believed that to enjoy a trip like this, one needed to accept, and even look forward to, these variables. Every day couldn't be a bluebird day, and every day was far too precious to waste being disgruntled.

We decided to head for a state park by Lake Bonaparte in the Okanogan/Wenatchee National Forest. This meant a six-mile detour for us, but Tex said the park was beautiful, with free camping and a decent road. Rolling in, we found it to be everything Tex promised. We claimed a peaceful site where we set up our tent on a cushy bed of pine needles donated by the towering ponderosa pines surrounding us. Lake Bonaparte was a crystal-clear lake that reflected the shimmering sunshine; ripples lapped the shores amid forested hillsides. Tucked in here, protected from the wind, we decided to take our first day off. After a week on the road, it felt wonderful to leisurely cook a breakfast of soup, scrambled eggs, grits, and hot chocolate. We took the time to hike around a bit and catch a nap in the middle of the day. As we started to clean up our bikes, we realized we needed a small brush to scrub off chains and derailleurs properly. Realizing that pine needles wouldn't cut it, we again improvised and decided we could get by with one toothbrush for the time being. Although this worked for us, I'd guess this might be where some might draw the line.

TAKING OUR TIME breaking camp the next morning we finally hit the road at about 9:30 with fresh legs. Our bikes were ready for the roads, thanks to a toothbrush and WD-40. Passing through the town of Republic, we started up Sherman Pass with an elevation of 5,570 feet, making it the highest pass in the state of Washington. We had reached that all-important point where we had become acclimated. We had caught our wind, so to speak, and unlike those first days, we now took in stride what the road put in front of us, accepting that this was to be our lifestyle for the time being.

We both felt strong heading up Sherman Pass, thanks in no small part to the rest day and extra food we had consumed. The next thing we knew, we had cleared the pass and—yee-haw—were met with 22 downhill miles and a strong tailwind! Dropping into the town of Kettle Falls, we decided to splurge on a restaurant. Although I realize some would shudder at the thought, we embraced a fat-filled meal of cheeseburgers and fries—and the chocolate malts weren't too shabby either.

In a bit of a food stupor, we hit the trail with the intent of getting a few miles closer to Idaho. Crossing Roosevelt Lake on a recently paved stretch of Hwy 395, we were stopped by a road-paving crew. After a brief wait, the flagger on our end gave us the okay to proceed. About a half mile ahead of us, we saw another flagger wildly waving arms. What the person was yelling was lost in the distance, but I guessed the yells weren't to cheer us on. As we neared, I could see that the flagger was a woman—one with an astounding variety of expletives—and it was now clear she was not cheering us on. I don't think she was having a good day, didn't like her job, or didn't realize that the first flagger had sent us through.

Some of her crew drove up from behind, and I had to ask, "What's up with Ms. Sunshine?" They laughed and replied, "You should have to work with her every day." Her verbal tirade continued as we passed her, and I couldn't help but share some of my own expletives gleaned from being raised by a World War II Navy veteran. Surprisingly, they shocked her into silence and she resorted to giving me a steely-eyed glare that could peel paint.

Just past Ms. Welcome Wagon, we arrived in Colville, a pretty little town about the size of the college town of River Falls, Wisconsin. With a quick pop into a grocery store to pick up some fruit and food for supper, we inquired about camping up the road. The man we spoke with was Mr. Don Running, a local photographer. After a round of when, where, how, and why questions about our trip, Don indicated that we would pass some farms down the road. He thought a farmer might allow us to pitch a tent for the night. What Don didn't tell us was that the climb out of town would be a hard, three-mile uphill push.

Neither of us was too thrilled when a car pulled up tight behind us and laid on the horn. It's always unnerving when a driver blows a horn on your tail. I was already struggling with the considerable miles logged and with going uphill on a fairly hot day, so my initial reaction was not one that would be appropriate for young children to witness. Even though bicyclists have legal rights to part of the road, legal doesn't mean a hoot if you end up with Goodyear Tiger Paw treads up your backside. Discretion is the better part of valor when responding to impatient motorists. All these thoughts clawed their way through my psyche in a nanosecond of startled surprise. We swerved, looked back, and saw Don Running waving through the windshield of the station wagon as he pulled up behind us.

"Oh, man, am I glad I found you guys. I got home and told my wife all about you and your trip and she was on me like white on rice about why I didn't invite you to spend the night with us." Don sputtered on about feeling terrible and apologized profusely for not thinking of it himself.

We looked uphill at what was still waiting to be climbed and before I could speak up, Denise accepted, "Don, we can't thank you enough. How do we get there?" Fortunately, Don's station wagon accommodated us—bikes, gear, and all. In that brief few minutes of backtracking, we went from a long climb ahead with an uncertain campsite and a minimal meal, to a beautiful home, comfortable beds, and a supper of steak and king crab. The Runnings were two of the most gracious hosts ever to welcome strangers into their home.

After a drill-holes-through-you hot shower, we enjoyed an incredible meal, during which Don and Eloise were kind enough to pretend they didn't notice we inhaled enough food for an army platoon. For the first half hour of dinner, we undoubtedly responded to every question with our mouths full. Afterward, lounging on a thick, carpeted living room floor, we enjoyed a great evening sharing stories. Eighty-five miles of biking, a hot shower, a tremendous dinner, and an ice cold beer, however, did not set the stage for a long evening of visiting. Denise and I were nodding off, and Don and Eloise were gracious enough to understand. I'm not sure if I was asleep before my head ever hit the pillow, but I do know that it ranked as one of my best night's sleep ever.

Arising at the uncharacteristically late hour of 8:00 A.M., we emerged to find that Eloise had washed our clothes and made a breakfast for royalty, with eggs, bacon, honeydew melon, and muffins. Don insisted we run to his store, where he took care of some camera issues we had. Finally, at 11:00 A.M., we prepared to leave. After we posed for pictures, gave hugs goodbye, and rolled down their driveway, we realized we left part of ourselves behind and carried with us their kindness and generosity in memories. Some people enter your life—even if for a brief period—and they leave a lasting impression, even 30 years later.

Closing in on Idaho, we were still caught up in the dilemma of traveling considerable miles north and/or south to make headway east. Biking in the mountains tended to keep us on somewhat more significant roadways than we intended. Most often, the "back roads" we had envisioned, although inviting, were also generally in much poorer shape and, more importantly, tended to have considerably steeper gradients. And so far, the traffic had been relatively light and the drivers courteous. Biking south on Highway 395 out of Colville, toward Loon Lake, we caught a back road to Highway 2 and headed toward Newport. Highway 2, at first glance on our maps, looked like it was going to be our home all the way across Idaho, Montana, and a good part of North Dakota.

We crossed paths with a father and son bicycling team on their way home to Seattle from Glacier National Park. Visiting briefly, we took time to glean information from one another about the conditions ahead. They recommended stopping at Pend Oreille State Park. Free camping and ten-cent hot showers sounded like just the ticket. Under a clear, star-filled sky that night, we realized that we'd be leaving Washington behind the following day and rolling into the panhandle of Idaho.

THE NEXT MORNING, after a quick 15 miles from Pend Oreille State Park, we arrived in Newport, where we stopped for breakfast. We had learned that, on many mornings, it actually made sense to eat our breakfast at a restaurant, for several reasons. First, almost every diner offered some great breakfast special at about $1.50. Not only would it have been difficult for us to cook eggs and toast, but we also wouldn't have been able to carry the extra eggs without breaking them. Second, we also avoided the whole issue of food preparation and cleanup time. This allowed us to quickly break camp in the morning, put on 15 to 20 or so miles when we were fresh, and then sit down for a break. The added bonus of a restroom with running water, although taken for granted by car travelers, was of immeasurable value to us.

Many times people were amazed that we would average 80 to 90 miles a day. Part of this disbelief stemmed from their perspective on biking, based on what they might have done. To many, the distance sounded impossible; however, although the miles were sometimes a bit of a push, we had all day. We enjoyed long periods of daylight and, with an early 15 to 20 miles before breakfast and another 20 to 30 miles before lunch, we had the remainder of the day—six or so hours—to complete another 40 or so miles. This allowed for a comfortable pace, breaks, and a chance to visit areas along the way. With each passing day, we became stronger and more fit, and extra pounds came off. The challenge then became consuming enough calories. We began to acquire that certain leanness—efficient, strong bodies. Although some might have thought we were skinny or maybe even starving, we were akin to rangy-looking, thin dogs that could run all day long and do it again tomorrow.

Having passed many Rainbow people the previous day, we were tempted to stop by their gathering, which was located just eight miles off our route. We had read an article that morning that local officials expected upward of 15,000 at the gathering, and after Tex's description, I thought it would have been a sight to see. Based on Tex's story, there would be at least a few thousand naked people dancing in a smoky haze. Then again, Tex was a worm rancher and may have been given to exaggeration. Although I'm sure the Rainbow folk would have welcomed us, we were looking forward to Idaho and Montana and decided to keep going.

Entering Idaho on Highway 2, we took a break for chocolate malts in Sandpoint. There is some beautiful wild country in northern Idaho, with plenty of room and few people. These northern areas seemed to grow people of an independent, leave-me-alone nature. The ones we met were friendly but also seemed to prefer keeping their space about them. We cut off of Highway 2 onto Highway 200, after being told it was less hilly. Skirting some mountains, we followed a river valley southeast to a town called Clark Fork. Stopping at a small diner, we were a little spooked by a large wanted poster for a man believed to be in the area. Evidently, he had recently murdered two Idaho Fish and Game wardens and was considered dangerous (ya think?).

With concerns about bad guys in such a remote area, we made a point to stop along the roadway where we could see both directions when it was time to camp. When the road was clear, we pulled our bikes into the woods, well out of sight of the road. By doing this, no one knew we were there, and we felt we could get a good night's rest without worry. Although we felt quite snug tucked back in the woods along the river, we also found ourselves the only meal in town for hoards of mosquitoes. We quickly boiled water to heat up turkey/gravy packs over bread and hit the hay, knowing we would enter "Big Sky country" Montana the following day.

WE MADE IT through the night at Clark Fork without being attacked by any wanted fugitives, although the mosquitoes forced a hasty retreat from our hideout campsite. After receiving some local advice—something like, "If you keep going on 200 you're heading into mountain roads that even local folks get lost on"—we decided to head north on Highway 56 to Highway 2, and then east to Libby, Montana.

On Highway 56, we had one of those experiences that set us back and really scared us. As we rode along, single-file on the far edge of the pavement, two logging trucks literally blew us off the road. The first truck had been traveling about 70 miles an hour and passed within inches of us. The second driver tried to get closer, even though the entire roadway was free of traffic in both directions. Despite our best efforts to ride safely, this was a moment when best efforts didn't matter, especially with drivers intent on threatening behavior. This last-second realization occurred as tons of metal rushed by within inches, preceded by a menacing wall of wind that caused my bike to shudder blowing me off the pavement to crash in the ditch. I picked myself up to see Denise in tears doing the same. If those gutless losers had been within reach, I have no doubt the world would be a better place right now. It was a shame because the vast majority of motorists were very good to us. We understood that although bicyclists sometimes abuse their use of the road by blocking traffic, the bottom line remains that a bicyclist cannot kill a driver, but bicyclists, on the other hand, can easily die, despite best efforts.

We pulled into Libby after a hot day and a close call, our nerves frayed. Fortunately, we found a free campground, but, unfortunately, some real characters were camped there. One group of six or eight had shaved heads and was clothed in body-length white robes. They pretty much kept to themselves, sat around their fire, and chanted something. The real spook was a guy wandering aimlessly and muttering about making deliveries one minute and about maggots on his body the next. Just a note: I never saw him deliver anything or saw any maggots on him when he tried to engage me. This guy was definitely on his own extended trip!

Apparently, Maggot Man had also freaked out a couple of young, 16- to 17-year-old guys from Kentucky who were on their own little road trip adventure; they asked if they could set up their tent next to ours. They were nice kids; their car had broken, and they were trying to figure out what to do. Their tent tight to ours, I felt like a mother hen but I didn't blame them for being scared.

With the Hare Krishnas or whoever they were chanting the night away, Maggot Man wandering about, and "our kids" tucked into their tent for the night, I reflected on the necessity of keeping guard. On a trip of this nature, we lived with certain vulnerabilities. Although I would never want to encase myself from all potential risks, I felt it was necessary to always keep a trick or two up the sleeve, no matter how friendly or nice a person may have seemed to be. The Idaho Fish and Game wardens' murderer, Maggot Man, and the white-robed chanters had not been part of what I envisioned for the trip, yet they seemed part of the package of the road less traveled.

CHAPTER 4

Glaciers, Grizzlies, and Horses

WITH LESS THAN a great night's sleep (always tough with one eye open), we beat an early path out of town. A bright sun rising on the horizon appeared to have driven our curious campmates into hiding, with neither a chant to be heard nor maggot to be seen. With a quick adios and good luck to the boys, we hit the road. Our goal had been to make 70 miles down Highway 2 to Marion, Montana. The traffic was light, but the road was rough with no paved shoulders. We kept a wary watch, as the area seemed to have a high population of "get out of my way" logging truck drivers.

Our maps showed only one town between Libby and Marion, a stretch of approximately 77 miles. This one town was called Traveler's Rest, and with nothing else in sight for 42 miles, we looked forward to it being our own traveler's rest stop. There are likely limited places in this country where one can travel such distances and not pass through some small community.

Along the way, we crossed paths with another bicyclist, and within minutes of visiting, I had no doubt that Brad was unique. Approaching one another from opposite directions, I wasn't initially sure what I was seeing. When we pulled up to one another, this guy cut quite a picture. Brad had shoulder-length blond hair, a days-old beard, and a typical ten-speed—none of which were too unusual. He was, however, pulling a two-wheeled "Bugger" trailer, and an eight-foot fishing pole was attached vertically behind his seat. At the risk of appearing and being nosy, I asked, "How is it dragging that trailer behind?" The question I wanted to ask: "What the heck you got in there?" Brad, friendly as could be, introduced himself and told us he was a bartender from Long Beach, California. While giving us his lowdown, he stamped out a cigarette butt and lit up a fresh one.

"Trailer pulls just great. When I'm biking, I like to bring along some comforts," he answered, proceeding to show us his radio, bath kit, pillow, French bread, beer, bowie knife, and—just "because you can't ever be too careful"—a .44 Mag revolver.

I asked, "How's the fishing been?" He indicated he hadn't used the pole yet, but believed it would come in handy somewhere on his 1,000-mile loop route. Figuring he might find himself in need of bait, I told him about Tex the worm rancher, and he seemed to absorb this information more seriously than I intended.

Before parting, I noted that he didn't seem to have a helmet. "Man, with all these logging trucks, do you wish you had a helmet along?" I asked.

"Nah, I figure if they hit me, great, because I'll just sue them and retire. I mean, I know it won't be a head-on and really, how far can a sideswipe throw you?"

Heading down the road, I couldn't help but think that Brad was one of those guys that could fall into a tank of piranhas and come out with a fish sandwich. The helmetless, chain-smoking, bartending bicyclist with a .44 Mag would likely live to be 100.

Continuing on, looking for the elusive Traveler's Rest, we encountered yet another cyclist. Mark—well equipped with front and rear panniers but no trailer or fishing rod—was certainly more traditional than Brad. With a long, full beard that had to catch a load of bugs in a full day on the road, he appeared very neat, organized, and capable. Mark had started his trip in Miami, Florida, biked up the East Coast to Maine, and was now headed home to Seattle, Washington. He had been on the road since February 1, and it was now July 1.

When long-distance bikers meet up, they invariably share information, particularly about the best food stop down the road. Mark gave us a heads-up for long-distance cuisine when he offered, "You know there is a little diner called Mike's Home Plate in a small town called Omro, Wisconsin, and trust me when I say they have the best pancakes I've ever had!" I couldn't believe my ears, because my hometown of Oshkosh,

Wisconsin, is only ten miles from Omro, and I had eaten at Mike's a couple of times. When I shared this with Mark, he asked if I had gone to North High School in Oshkosh, because he had camped there one night. It was, in fact, my high school. We wished Mark a safe trip as he finished up his 6,000-mile ride, and went our separate ways.

Having seen no homes, stores, or towns for 40 miles, we were a bit eager to arrive at the town of Traveler's Rest. Five miles up the road, we found Traveler's Rest, but were surprised: I guess placing a bar and restaurant called Traveler's Rest on the map is acceptable when there are no other towns for 80 miles. That was it, just a wide spot in the road, but nonetheless offered food, beverages, and a bathroom. All things considered, that seemed to cover most of our needs those days.

Nearing Marion, we intended to camp on the outskirts when a local guy pulled up and offered information about recent bear problems in the area. Uncertain if he had been jerking our chain or not, we decided to push on for an hour and made camp just outside of Kalispell, in the shadow of the Rocky Mountains west of Glacier National Park.

ON AN EXTENDED bike trip, daily activities leave a person feeling like Bill Murray in the movie *Groundhog Day*. One falls into a routine of making camp, cooking, sleeping, breaking camp, and riding, and repeating this scenario. As the trip unfolded, the days passed and the scenery changed, as did we. Some days we felt the road pulling us along, leaving us anxious to see around the next curve; other days, we just felt like stopping. The environment drove some of this; other times, we were just having "one of those days." Either way, it was important for us to pay attention to what our mood and body were telling us. If we hadn't, we might have become candidates for physical problems or mental burnout—either of which might have been game breakers for our trip. As the miles rolled by, stretching out our mileage goals became tempting; however, we found we could lose sight of the present time if we kept looking ahead to tomorrow and beyond. To prevent this, we built in "off" days, and with Glacier National Park just up the road, we decided an off day—without bikes—was in order.

ON JULY 2ND, we covered the 40 miles to Glacier, and must have stopped at every souvenir, rock, and pawn shop on the road. Buying nothing, we had a great day being tourists. Grabbing the opportunity to hit a bike shop in Kalispell, we picked up a new tire and replaced a chain. We knew the plains east of the Rockies would offer little in bike repair. I also bought a 12-inch American flag on a two-foot stick that sat behind my bike seat. Although my intent was to celebrate the upcoming Fourth of July, I noticed that not only were drivers giving us a wider berth, but they were also friendlier. I guess I'd found something of a commonality with even the truck drivers who also seemed to be more respectful of our space.

Pulling into Apgar Campground in West Glacier, we found that no sites were available, something we should have anticipated with the holiday. Once again, we were blessed by the kindness of strangers—Bert and Martha Pices, who offered to share their campsite with us. Bert and Martha were both in their 60s, and had biked here from Spokane, Washington. Their children and grandchildren were to arrive by car the following day. Grateful for their generosity, we set up camp and hiked over to Lake McDonald.

Lake McDonald was absolutely stunning, from its crystal-clear water to the incredible mountains that surround it. This was not to say Glacier National Park was not commercial-ized, as was evident from the park restaurant and rowboats available for rent. But although this was a ride-up/drive-up campground, the park also had miles and miles of wilderness laced with hiking trails. These various paths of exploration addressed the needs of the diverse populations and their dif-ferent perspectives of the perfect vacation. Denise and I con-sidered ourselves pretty "outdoorsy" and rough and ready, however, I would be lying if I said we didn't enjoy the pizza at the restaurant the previous night, or for that matter, the running water and restrooms. For those who prefer the purity of a WhisperLite stove for their meals and like to dig a hole for their potty needs, more power to them. I would like to believe that, if we're being honest, most of us find our-selves somewhere in the middle, and to this end, the National Park Service has done an exceptional job of planning for multiple uses of our recreational areas. It's sometimes easy to take things for granted, and we need to always remind ourselves to count our blessings for the beautiful parks we enjoy in the United States.

Walking the shoreline past beautiful rowboats, I spun around at the sound of a splash behind me. I couldn't believe my eyes as Denise broke the surface with a loud "yikes" and a shiver I felt on shore. As she staggered back to land, she exclaimed, "Thatttt felllttt realllly gooood." I had my doubts. Looking at the snow-covered mountains ringing Lake McDonald, I stuck my fingers in the water and felt a bone-numbing sensation that transcended the word *cold*. Miss "Felt Really Good" raced to pull on her shed sweatshirt and pants, and if I believed her, the uncontrollable shaking and goose bumps had just been due to the excitement of the moment because "the water wasn't too bad."

A water lover my whole life, I suggested we enjoy the lake *on* the surface. So, for the next hour, we plied the waters of this beautiful lake with Queen Denise lounging in the stern while her galley slave Bob took to the oars. It truly was a beautiful day, and as we returned the boat, we realized that places like this demanded more than just one day off, so we decided to stay two.

Back at the Park Service station, we explored other options available on a limited budget. I bought an interesting, if gruesome, book called *Night of the Grizzlies,* a story about a horrible incident that occurred several years earlier when a grizzly bear attacked and killed two college-age girls while they camped in East Glacier Park. That story made me look forward to a nice night's sleep in a tent!

Denise, in the meantime, made another discovery: "Hey, we can rent horses and ride as part of a group up to Sperry Chalet above the tree line in the mountains!" Denise loved horses, having owned one as a young girl, but this was truly a point where she and I had divergent viewpoints about what was fun. All of my previous experiences on horses had led me to believe horseback riding was a penance of sorts and was meant to be painful. My bike saddle was a joy in comparison to a real saddle, and I have never experienced a more solid thud than that experienced upon being launched out of a saddle to the ground.

Fortunately for Denise, our relationship then was still in those early starry-eyed times. It should be no surprise that, in that state of mind, I replied, "Yeah, that would really be neat." I don't care how many guys read this and snicker, because I know if they are honest, they would all recall one or more of their own personal versions of this scenario in the early times of a romance.

Next thing I knew, I was holding the reins of "Dudley," my horse for the day. In the meantime, Denise was almost giddy with excitement about this new plan. Dudley looked me over in my wool biking shorts, and I couldn't help but notice his size—his rear end appeared to be about two axe handles wide. I'm sure we both had our own versions of the thought, "No way, Jose." At the same time, Denise, the young, good-looking biker girl, seemed to have more than her share of attention from a crew of young cowboy wranglers. Giving her stirrups undivided attention, apparently they didn't find it problematic that my left knee was under my chin while my right foot dangled free. No matter how good a guy might be in the self-confidence department, there's something about good-looking, rangy cowboy types that can make a guy in wool shorts feel inadequate, particularly with women around. You know, that kind of feeling Billy Crystal had around Curly in the movie *City Slickers*.

Grudgingly agreeing that my stirrups needed to at least be in the same universe, the cowboys made the adjustment and we were off up the trail. I had to admit it started as a fun and beautiful ride. Of course, this might have reflected that early time in a relationship that I mentioned previously. For the first half hour, I had a good time. True, Dudley's girth splayed my legs out in a manner more suited to a high school cheerleader doing the splits, and my butt rubbed hard on the saddle, but what the heck, this was fun, right?

Two hours later, as we passed through snowbanks and the last of the trees, I started to think a stone wedge coated in sandpaper had replaced my saddle. Fortunately, we had gone as far as possible due to the snow. The prospect of walking this last part became a welcomed thought—until I tried to get off the beast. As I tried to dismount, pain radiated through my body. Just at that moment, Mr. I'm a Cowboy Stud swaggered by, leaving me no option but to hide my misery, jump down from Dudley, and exclaim, "I thought this would be hard, but it was a piece of cake." From the look of pity on Denise's face and the sly chuckle from Mr. CS, it was obvious neither was buying it. Planting my butt for a moment on an icy snowbank (wet or not, it felt like heaven), we climbed a trail to Sperry Chalet.

Celebrating the Fourth of July at the top of the Rocky Mountains, the incredible views looking down the long valley and ending in Lake McDonald were spectacular.

Sperry Chalet was an all-stone restaurant and lodge. Everything needed to build it, as well as for its daily operation, had to be hauled up on horseback. A woman named Rose ran Sperry Chalet, and she oversaw a crew of young women who worked there in the summer, serving us pie, ice cream, and a beverage that really hit the spot after the ride up. The girls were from all around the country, and they loved it. They explained that Rose only allowed them down the mountain if they could make the round trip in one day, which tended to keep them up at the chalet almost all summer. Rose was like everybody's grandma, and she and her crew made everyone feel very welcome.

The terrain was rugged with mountains and precipitous drops all around us, perfect for the half dozen snow-white mountain goats in our immediate vicinity. They certainly were not tame, but being accustomed to people, they allowed us a few nice camera shots.

Although some people in our group had planned to stay the night and ride down the next day, the rest of us made a one-day round trip of it. On the way back to our horses, we couldn't help but take the time to have our first-ever snow-ball fight on the Fourth of July. I called for a truce when the last one spattered against the back of my head, although I managed to catch Denise with one last shot just as we reached Dudley and company. I had been really dreading the return trip, but then I started to think about going downhill and I figured it couldn't be too bad. What was I thinking?

As sure-footed Dudley negotiated the rough, steep down-hill terrain, the hell saddle undulated from side to side and up and down as his back and feet adjusted for the terrain. My previously numb butt was once again alive with pain, but with a new dimension of misery added to my knees as they fought gravity to hold me up in the saddle. Just in case this physical agony was not enough, I couldn't imagine what I looked like to those behind me as my body rolled, shifted, and undulated from side to side with the swaying of Dudley. My stomach began to roll and flip-flop like a Slinky as my pie and ice cream thought about an encore.

Two hours later, back at the home corral, Denise bid adieu to her cowboy buddies and Dudley and I shared a look of good riddance. Treating ourselves to a large pizza and pitcher of cold beer that night, I now knew how good a meal tasted after surviving a battle. Fighting off sleep, we made it back to our tent. As I slipped into a deep snooze, I wondered how I would survive many more of Denise's rest days.

FEELING SURPRISINGLY REFRESHED the next morning, we decided to get an early start up the Going-to-the-Sun Road to Logan Pass. We'd been told the traffic becomes heavy and that this route was steep and difficult. Although this was supposed to be a rest day, I figured a mountain pass by bike would be a piece of cake compared to Dudley's fat back for six hours. Saying good-bye to Bert and his family we started the climb amid some of the most spectacular scenery in North America.

We rode in awe of the snowcapped peaks, past tall cascading waterfalls and lush green valleys full of tufts of beargrass, and arrived at Logan Pass surprised that the "tough climb" was done. Although a hike, it had been much easier than the Smokey Mountain passes of the previous year or Allison or Sherman Pass in Canada. Wildflowers bloomed in the roadside and tall snowbanks melted across the roadway as we strapped on our helmets for an incredible high-speed, winding bike flight into East Glacier by St. Mary.

Setting up camp that night, we were aware that we had exceeded our daily budgets for this point in the trip, but we had been told three times that we had to eat at Johnson's Café in St. Mary. For $5.00, the family-style all-you-can-eat dinner of chicken, soup, mashed potatoes, coleslaw, and ice cream could not be beat. I doubt the Johnson family came out on top of the deal with me at the table. On our way back to camp, we picked up a small bag of Oreo cookies. As we looked up at clouds gathering near Logan Pass, a cool breeze lifted and a light drizzle began to fall, pushing us inside our tent for the evening.

Rain drummed on the outside of the tent, but the warm feeling of being secure inside engulfed us both as we burrowed into warm sleeping bags. Reflecting on the last two weeks, it seemed hard to believe the experiences we'd had so far. I think we both had answered for ourselves what had been an unspoken question: How would we get along and function together? Anyone who has ever embarked on a trip with another person, particularly a 4,000-mile bike trip, knows that there will be daily challenges. The ability to work together and adapt is crucial to an enjoyable, successful experience. A simple analogy would be to experience even a day trip in a canoe with another person. I can't prove this, but I would wager more than one relationship has ended somewhere between putting in and taking out a canoe. Dealing with all those "Whose fault is it we hit the rock?" sort of issues can really jeopardize any canoe trip and certainly tax any relationship. The same holds true on a long-distance bike trip, and evidently, Denise and I were well suited to working together because we had not experienced any issues in which we found ourselves under each other's skin. Denise was incredible. She was extremely competent in bike mechanics, and she had core strength, both physical and mental, that helped her overcome any obstacle thrown at her. She daily pushed through those inevitable small and big obstacles—from flat tires to long, difficult climbs to unending rain.

"How does the road ahead look?" she drowsily inquired.

Glancing at our map, it was easy to see that we would be leaving mountains behind and begin a long segment across the plains the following day.

"Well, we're sure as heck not going to be using the gears on our bikes like we did in the mountains. From here on out, it's flat as a pancake for a long way."

I knew we undoubtedly would have some hills and mountains the following day, but we were headed back to Highway 2, which we would travel across Montana. Our days of riding 80 miles to make 40 miles of eastward progress were behind us. Highway 2 was a straight shot east through northern Montana, and if the westerly winds prevailed, we would most likely start putting in some big-mile days and finally be traveling "as the crow flies."

Denise had fallen asleep while I finished my journal entry and munched a couple of Oreos. I knew we weren't supposed to have food in the tent as we were in bear country and, in fact, in the same vicinity of the bear attack recounted in *Night of the Grizzlies,* which I had just completed. However, with the rain and stupid rationalization that "It would never happen to me," I brought the cookies in with me. I clicked off my light, warm and safe with a full belly of Johnson's Café home cooking. Falling into a deep slumber, I dreamt of down the road.

I AWOKE WITH a jolt as the corner of the tent by my head was pushed into me. In a second, I scrambled out of my bag and crouched in the small tent. I heard the bear right outside through the nylon fabric. In a millisecond, I kicked myself repeatedly for being so stupid to have brought the Oreos inside with me. With my legs folded under me and starting to cramp, and every fiber of my body screaming, I clutched my pocket knife in one hand and a small spray can of mace in the other. With the sounds of the bear breathing, prodding, and pushing against the tent doorway, I knew I had to do something quickly. In my heart, I knew the small knife would be useless against a grizzly bear, and the mace was intended for use on human problems. As thoughts of the gruesome scenario from *Night of the Grizzlies* ran through my head, I fought not to panic.

The best I could come up with was to use the knife to cut the tent on the opposite end, whereby Denise and I would dive out the hole and attempt to climb a tree directly behind us. With little time to spare, I realized that I must first awaken Denise (that's right, she slept soundly through this). I also realized I would have to do so quietly so as not to scare her and provoke what, up to now, seemed only a hungry and curious bear. Before cutting the tent, I quietly reached for Denise's feet, intending to gently and quietly shake her awake. With the now louder breathing of the bear right beside me and every fiber of my body ready to explode, I reached down for her feet. With a start and a yell, Denise sat up as my fingers poked into her face. With the moment as tense as it was, I responded with my own startled shout. Like a scene out of a *Three Stooges* episode—with yells, a tousle, twisting sleeping bags, and thumping tent walls—it took me a few seconds to find my light, look at a now terrified Denise, and realize what had happened.

When I first awoke with a start, I had twisted myself around in the pitch-dark tent. Although I thought I was at the door end of the tent, I was actually on the opposite end. With the help of an overactive imagination, the "grizzly" nighttime reading, and the Double Stuf Oreos at my side, I created a worst-case scenario in my head. What about the heavy breathing? Seeing how I had spun myself around in the tent, I was hearing *Denise's* breathing the whole time, along with a curious raccoon bumping the tent outside, which had caused me to manufacture my own version of *Night of the Grizzlies.*

As my body fibers gelled into that feeling we experience after a real or (in my case) perceived close call, Denise looked at me like maybe she should reevaluate her confidence in me. I thanked God that I decided to shake Denise's foot *before* I slashed the tent and made a dive for the tree. With a few more very feeble comments, I tried unsuccessfully to convince Denise that I had not overreacted, and we both settled back in and managed to sleep a few hours before dawn.

I UNZIPPED THE tent door the next morning, grateful I was not crawling through a large cut, and decided my first order of business was to throw away *that* book and a now-empty Oreo package. As Denise emerged from the tent, I took a stab at damage control by greeting her with, "Boy, did you ever have a bad dream last night. Do you even remember me waking you up to calm you?"

With a look that said far more than simply "nice try," she made me realize that, short of her suffering a case of amnesia, I was going to pay for this for some time.

CHAPTER 5

New Friends and Flatland

AFTER ALMOST TWO WEEKS of battling mountains, we anticipated being spit out onto the vast plains, chased full speed by tailwinds pushing us to 140-mile days. Heading out of St. Mary we immediately encountered a killer, six-mile climb—the mountains weren't done chewing on us yet. The climb probably wasn't that bad, but we had set ourselves up for a little disappointment, having wrapped our minds around hitting flat plains. Amid this adversity, however, we encountered another bicyclist by the name of Dale Reiber, whom we would end up sharing the road with for the next two weeks. Dale was a special education teacher from Arizona, as well as the owner of a small bike shop, and he was also on a bike trip across country. He was headed to Maine, and would head north into Canada around the Great Lakes when we would veer south. His trip was part of a fundraiser for the Special Olympics, and he had acquired sponsorship pledges for $145,000.

At the top of the climb, we began a long, curving descent out of the last of the mountains. Hills, mountains, curves, and forests had surrounded us for the past two weeks. Now, as we rounded one last curve, we were treated to views of vast, wide-open, level plains that stretched before us. When Denise exclaimed, "I think I can see the trees in Minnesota," I knew exactly what she meant: The view that we rode into that day made clear Montana's description as "Big Sky country." The abrupt transition of surroundings was almost a visual shock—flat plains joined with a seemingly endless ocean of blue sky.

We rolled into the flatlands town of Browning, Montana, and with the instincts of long-distance bikers, stopped at a local bakery. Over donuts, we met local resident Henry Boyle, a member of the Blackfeet tribe who was kind enough to take us for a brief visit to the Museum of the Plains Indian, as well as to the studio of renowned western artist Bob Schriver. I didn't need to be an art expert to appreciate the ability this man had to capture bronze scenes of the land through which we were riding.

Leaving Browning behind, we headed dead east and rode incredible tailwinds that grabbed our butts and pushed us down the road at an easy 25 MPH clip. Despite the long, slow morning climb and the great visits with Henry and the Browning tourist stops, we blew into Shelby with a 90-mile day under our belts. Right when we thought the day couldn't get any better, we rolled into a campground with a community pool and hot showers. With the mountains behind us, the plains ahead, and a new friend along, life was looking good. We'd had our ups and downs, literally and figuratively, and certainly more awaited us, but I realized how many incredible possibilities awaited us if we would just take the time to bike a new path through life.

WHIPPED ALONG BY the wind, surrounded by miles of open prairie, I understood better what pioneers must have felt. It reminded me of a musical I saw once, called "Rough and Ready," that took place in a western town in the 1800s. In it, one of the songs celebrates living: "Where the wind blows free / That's the place I want to be."

Joining up with Dale had been great, but he wasn't the only addition to our group: Last I had heard, some called the wind "Mariah," and she was definitely along for the ride. She appeared to be blustery from time to time, occasionally blowing her cool and voicing her opinion with a moan or a whistle. She could be friend or foe, but one thing was certain: She was in a big hurry and really kept us moving all day.

I thought that the wind blew a lot in Wisconsin, but with the air pressure changes occurring on the east side of the Rockies and a thousand miles of unimpeded plains, the wind howled in Montana. If one happened to be traveling in the same direction, it was tailwind heaven. Conversely, I pitied those trying to ride *into* the breath of this beast. In no time, we found our big gears spinning effortlessly, the wind propelling us down the highway at speeds of 35+ MPH. Engulfed in Mariah's embrace as we were, we heard minimal sound until we'd passed under a power line. Here the wind and power line did battle for the air space, both combining to emit a loud, low moan that briefly surrounded us until Mariah triumphed and whisked us on again.

At one point, I decided I wanted to put on my windbreaker in the somewhat cool morning temperature. Telling Denise and Dale that I'd catch up, I stopped to pull out my jacket. Standing in the middle of Highway 2 with no cars in sight and surrounded by mile upon mile of empty prairie, I struggled with my furiously flapping jacket in wind gusts of up to 60 MPH. Amid the vastness, I contemplated how this was truly a lonely place. I couldn't help but again think of the early pioneers who had chosen this area to homestead. With few trees available, many had constructed sod huts in which they attempted to survive their first winter. One could stand here and imagine the loneliness and even fear that might have engulfed these families, many with children, as they attempted to establish a life on these plains. The winters had to be horrific, as blizzards swept unimpeded across the land and past these homesteads, and the families often had no one to depend on but one another.

As I finally secured my jacket and contemplated these thoughts of loneliness and hardship, I realized how far I had fallen behind. Denise and Dale were not even in sight, and I suddenly felt I was alone in the world, as alone as I had ever felt in my life, as alone as those settlers must have felt surrounded by the emptiness of the plains. In an almost frantic moment, I kicked down the gears, quickly reached over

35 MPH, and caught up to them within minutes as they slowed for me.

With the tailwinds, we breezed through the small towns of Chester, Joplin, and Rudyard along Highway 2—one of the most desolate main highways in the United States. We were only about 35 miles south of Canada, and I was certain the horizon I saw to the north sat under the maple leaf flag. Tumbleweeds of various sizes rolled along the plains beside us until they encountered barriers that caused them to pile up.

We stopped in Havre, the largest town around for many miles, bought groceries for an evening meal, and headed to a wayside we had heard about, hoping to make it our campsite. The wind had continued to increase, with gusts that reportedly reached 60 MPH. Sailing into the wayside at breakneck speed, we tossed out an anchor to stop, but quickly realized we would have no way to cook dinner, much less pitch tents, in these blustery conditions. Looking for options, I scouted out a gravel pit a short distance down the road, thinking the pit might provide some protection. I walked down into the pit, and looked up to see Denise and Dale laughing as I shielded my eyes from the stinging gravel and airborne dust swirling around me. There was no way this was going to work!

"You looked like the astronaut's picture on the surface of the moon," Dale shouted to me.

From the sheer desolation of that gravel pit, I couldn't help but imagine this area as a candidate for future astronaut survival training. Other than the oxygen, everything else created the perfect lunar surface.

Hopping on our bikes, we continued down the highway, the miles rapidly passing beneath us as we sought other options. It wasn't long before we encountered a neat, white farm home with a shelter belt of trees providing some protection from the wind. Stopping to knock on the door, we were greeted by Mr. and Mrs. Wallace and Lillian Rolf and their sons, Wade and Wynne. We introduced ourselves and told them of our trip, explaining our dilemma and asking if we might set up our tents behind their shelter trees. Once again, strangers opened their lives—and their lawn—to us.

Even in the shelter of the trees, the wind seemed merciless. We struggled to erect our tents as they flapped like flags. Anything not weighted down was lost at a speed that even Lance Armstrong couldn't ride down. With dogged diligence, we finally raised and staked down our tents, though the wind continued to infiltrate any tiny opening to inflate them like bloated bike tubes. Late in the day, we were finally able to cook a meal, and eat rapidly as darkness closed in. We crawled into the tents and out of the wind as it moaned throughout the evening in its struggle through the trees.

The wind maintained a steady roar through the night; in fact, I was amazed the trees withstood the pressure. The Rolf family invited us in for breakfast the next morning and, as they welcomed us into their home like family, I experienced an odd, uncomfortable moment when something didn't feel right. Sitting down, I realized it was the absolute stillness, the quietness, the absence of wind slashing across my skin—something I hadn't experienced in the past two days. Any wariness quickly evaporated as we dug into a huge breakfast of French toast, eggs, and ham. The Rolfs are one of those solid families with that inherent toughness necessary to survive out on the plains yet at the same time with a soft spot and helping hand for passing strangers. When on the road, I found these encounters fueled us every bit as much as the meals they shared. With work awaiting the Rolfs and miles ahead of us, we bid farewell, pointed our bikes east, and set sail on a wicked tailwind.

Back on Highway 2, we rolled along like the tumbleweeds on either side of us. Fences lined both sides of the highway, and we soon came upon a small herd of 15 to 20 open-range cattle. As we approached them, they spooked and stampeded east along the south side of the highway. Suddenly taking a hard left, they barreled full tilt through the barbed-wire fence and up onto the highway, charging ahead of us. As we slowed, they again veered left off the highway and tore right through the north fence line. Coming to a full stop we watched them head north until we lost sight of all but a cloud of dust in their wake. Although this action was exciting, we couldn't imagine how the rancher would ever find his "lost doggies." Then again, for all we knew, the same rancher might very well own 10 or 20 square miles on both sides of the road.

UP TO THIS point, we had been having good luck as far as the mechanics of our bikes. Other than Denise's tire slash on day one, we'd experienced no problems. While packing that morning, Dale had commented, "One thousand plus miles and not even a flat."

"Knock on wood," I'd replied, remembering well the number of spokes I had replaced on my Florida trip.

Soon we had put on 80 miles and began crossing the Belknap Reservation. Passing through a marshy area, we were met with another kind of stampede of the biggest, fastest, hardiest mosquitoes we've ever experienced, and that means a lot coming from a Wisconsinite. When these babies were done sucking our blood, we felt like we needed transfusions! As the skeeters swarmed me, I got my first flat, and despite changing it in a time that would impress an Indy 500 pit crew, I fed dozens of these pterodactyl-sized mosquitoes. We were no sooner rolling again when I heard a loud whoosh from behind me, as Dale flatted on a worn-through tire. Ten minutes and about 100 bites apiece later, we were back rolling east. Not 20 minutes later, I was startled to hear the dreaded *ping* of a broken spoke. Fortunately, it was not on the freewheel side, and I quickly trued my wheel, and we headed on again.

We had hoped to make it as far as Glasgow that day, but thanks to Dale and me setting ourselves up by bragging about our good fortune with bike mechanics, we came up a bit short. Instead, we decided to make camp at a rest area about 15 miles shy of Glasgow. Despite this, we had still traveled an incredible 136 miles for the day. We pulled into a rest area, where we met a couple from Oregon who gave us three ice-cold PBRs (Pabst Blue Ribbons) and boy, did they slide down nicely.

As we set up camp, a Winnebago pulled in right next to us, and I mean right next to us, as close as 5 to 10 feet. The elderly couple driving it stepped out and introduced themselves as Phil and Gracie. They were 80 years old, and were covering a route for Phil's sales. Friendly as could be, it was obvious that they had knocked back a few brews before coming to a stop for the day. They invited us inside for dinner, and not being the type to pass up a good deal, we gave them our best Midwestern "you betcha."

Before we could sit down, we each had an ice-cold JR Ewing beer in our hands.

"We've leap-frogged you kids two times now on this highway, and when we saw you camped, Gracie said we just have to give those kids a dinner."

Gracie plopped down tight next to me and started rubbing my leg while slurring, "You sure have some nice strong legs."

Glimpsing a smirk on Denise's face, I thought, *What the hell, I can handle this, at least until we get fed.*

Gracie unclenched my knee and got busy at the stove while Phil brought out some of the products he sells.

"Yeah, these babies are really a hot ticket," he claimed, pulling out a deck of playing cards, each sporting a different voluptuous topless young lady.

"But I gotta show you my best seller." As he dug into a cabinet, I was ready for anything and wouldn't have been surprised if he'd pulled out a blow-up doll. To all of our surprise, he turned around with a large (I'm talking a one-foot-long) plastic housefly.

"Yeah, these babies are hot right now," Phil beamed, handing it off to Denise with all the care of a grandfather passing off his grandbaby.

Gracie was now back with three more JR Ewings and, with her radar focused this time on Dale's appendages, I was able to sit back, relax, and enjoy my beer without being groped. In the meantime, Phil had cozied up next to Denise and was showing off his giant flyswatter that "is a natural once you've sold them some flies."

Following a dinner of giant frankfurters (probably a favorite of giant flies), we gently extricated ourselves from the Winnebago as Phil and Gracie wound down to a stupor.

As we crawled into our tent only six feet away, we could hear Phil and Gracie through their open window.

Phil said, "That Denise. Now she's a real honey."

Gracie replied, "I liked those strong legs on those boys, but dammit, I didn't intend to have them eat and drink us out of house and home."

As they continued to banter back and forth about us, I had to admit I felt a little guilty having had a good meal and a few brews. I mentioned this to Denise, and she reminded me that Gracie did get to squeeze my leg. With that unpleasant reminder and a shudder, I was off to sleep with a clear conscience.

WANTING TO HIT the road before Phil and Gracie were up and about, we broke camp quickly and quietly, and headed for Glasgow. We pedaled only about 20 miles before we hit town and pulled in for a bakery stop. Here, we learned of Fort Peck Lake Reservoir and Recreation Area just 20 miles south of Highway 2. We decided we would enjoy a day off from biking at Fort Peck Lake. We stocked up on taco fixings before leaving Glasgow, and were soon camped on a hill overlooking the lake. This large body of water—rare for this area—was made possible by damming the Missouri River, the largest earthen dam in the world at the time it was built. Earlier we passed through Glasgow, and I had seen some larger water ski–type boats. I had wondered where a person would ever use one around here. Now I knew, and judging from the number of people there, it was obvious that this area was a magnet for folks looking for a break from the otherwise dry, dusty plains.

As the three of us stretched out and relaxed on the shores of this oasis on the prairie, Gary and Roxanne Funk saw our bikes and gear and approached to ask Denise and me where we came from. As we filled in the blanks to their questions, they became more intrigued and asked if we could ride into Wolf Point the following day to be their guests at the opening night of the Wolf Point Rodeo. They gave us a time and place to meet, and we said we'd do our best to make it. We headed back to camp to discuss this latest opportunity with Dale, and found that Dale had also rustled up a little side-action waterskiing for us the following day. As we settled into an afternoon of tacos and a couple of cold ones, we all agreed the rodeo sounded too good to miss. Unfortunately, this meant we would have to pass on the waterskiing offer. Life is tough, and sometimes we just have to make hard decisions. As long as this rodeo had no expectations of me sitting on a horse I was sure I would enjoy it!

That evening, we shared a campfire and looked out over the plains, the lake, and the setting sun. As we shared stories about home, it was obvious that Dale was a bit homesick and very definitely missed his wife Louise back in Arizona. I felt that Dale perhaps envied the opportunity Denise and I had to share our experiences on the road, and I knew he would have given anything for Louise to be there with us at that moment. We realized that we were doing something that many people would never get the chance to do, or if they had the chance, would never take it. We each had a life down the road at the end of this trip, but we knew we would carry people we'd met and moments like that night with us for the rest of our lives.

CHAPTER 6

Rodeos and Roughnecks

THE NEXT MORNING, the air was cool, the sky was clear, and the wind blew right into our faces at 30 MPH as we began our backtrack north to where we had left Highway 2 the day before. For all the incredible tailwinds we had enjoyed the past few days, we were now paying the piper in spades. We formed into a three-person draft line, whereby bikers line up tight behind one another like birds in flight. The person up front bears the brunt of a brutal headwind, thereby giving those behind a break. When the front biker tires, he drops back to the end of the line; in this fashion, we slowly leapfrogged ahead. After ten torturous miles, we realized we would never make it to Wolf Point on time for the rodeo. We stopped for a short break along the road, and Dale threw out his thumb in a mock hitchhiking gesture to a passing semi-trailer. Much to our surprise, the truck pulled to the side and came to a stop. As we approached the semi, which was pulling a full-size mobile home for delivery, the driver stepped down from his cab. Figuring this guy was going to be pissed off for stopping, we explained what we were up to.

He surprised us again, saying, "Oh, hell, I do a little biking, and I know what these winds can be like. Go ahead and climb in the mobile home with your bikes and I'll at least get you back to Highway 2 before I head west."

Needing only a brief time to consider his offer, we knew this would be the only way we would make Wolf Point on time. My only hesitation was that I had made a commitment to myself that I would not accept rides on this trip, but as Dale pointed out, we were purely backtracking to where we had turned off. That simple rationalization worked for me.

Next thing we knew, we were in someone's future kitchen holding our bikes. It was certainly a different perspective as I parted the window curtains over the sink and contemplated the passing scenery. This was definitely one way to deal with headwinds! Rattling down the highway, shouting to be heard, we shared a laugh at the absurdity of what we were doing. I stood over the stove watching the tumbleweeds and scenery fly by, joking with Dale and Denise: "How would you like your eggs this morning?"

Despite the fun we were having with this scenario, we prayed we would not be the brunt of this guy's joke, hoping he didn't plan to dump us back in the state of Washington on the West Coast. In a matter of 15 minutes, we felt the house slowing down and pulling over. With a bit of the same trepidation of Dorothy and Toto, we cautiously opened the door of the house, uncertain of where we had landed. We saw no witch crushed beneath us, but rather Highway 2, our own version of the Yellow Brick Road, stretched out in front of us. With handshakes and waves, we parted company with our fellow biker/trucker and headed separate ways. Once again catching a bit of a tailwind, we rolled into Wolf Point on time. After our surreal semi ride, we figured the strangeness of the day was behind us. Not by a long shot!

If someone had told me that, in the span of about 48 hours, an 80-year-old lady would squeeze my leg, a semi would pull Denise, Dale, and our bikes down the highway in a mobile home, and we'd all be preparing to ride our bikes in a rodeo parade in Wolf Point, Montana, I would have wondered what—and how much—they were smoking!

When we met up with Gary and Roxanne, they were ready for us, complete with signs for our bikes that identified us as cross-continent bike trippers. The entire town turned out for this event, and judging from the festive atmosphere surrounding us, rodeos in Montana ranked right up there with the Fourth of July. We fell into place behind a group of rodeo dignitaries on horseback, and paraded through town, dodging the numerous piles of horse apples in our path. Weaving through town and waving like Shriners, we were definitely caught up in the excitement. Soon, we felt a little like celebrities, with people approaching us and asking about our trip. We even had a chance to dance a bit with some cancan dancers (add that to the "could this day be any weirder?").

Arriving at the rodeo that evening we were introduced to the crowd. Gary Funk galloped into the arena on horseback, carrying the Montana state flag and bringing everyone to their feet. This was one of those days that seemed to never end—in a good way. At midnight we loaded our bikes into Gary's horse trailer and headed out to his "little spread." A late-night snack of ice cream and Oreo cookies hit the spot before we hit the hay. As I dozed off to sleep, Oreos by my side, I knew there would be no bear attacks to worry about.

THE NEXT MORNING, it was pretty clear that the Funk family was not about to let us head down the road with anything less than a belly full of bacon, eggs, toast, waffles, juice, and more. These were definitely my kind of people. Joining us that morning was Gary's dad, Dave, and I don't think one could find a more "salt of the earth" kind of person. Visiting with Dave felt like visiting with true Montana and all I imagined Big Sky country to be about. He was a cowboy, rancher, family man and, as a bonus, a musician— treating us to a song on his concertina. Dave walked and talked with his feet planted firmly on the ground and his legs a bit bowlegged from more than a few years in the saddle. He had a look in his eye that said there wasn't much he didn't understand.

While Denise continued to sleep, Gary had asked me, "Do you guys want to ride out on horseback to see the ranch and cattle?" I thanked God that Denise was still asleep, as memories of Dudley and the saddle sores sent shudders through me. Feeling a bit like I did around the young cowboy wranglers at Glacier, I tried to rustle up my own swagger.

With a bit of a drawl I replied, "I appreciate the offer, Gary, because I've spent a few hours in the saddle myself," and with a wink, added, "But you know, and don't tell her I said this, but Denise is just a little tuckered out and I don't know if she would be up to it."

Sharing one of those knowing looks that pass between men when they know they are looking out for their women folk, we gave each other a nod and settled on taking the truck. Once again, quick thinking averted another potential disaster!

As we drove across the prairie into the vast Montana sky, I asked when we would get to the ranch. Gary replied, "We're on it."

Their little spread was about 2,000 acres, and Gary insisted it really was of modest size. Coming from Wisconsin where many farms are a hundred acres, I thought this seemed huge; however, to graze black Angus cattle, ranchers needed much more space than is required for dairy cattle.

After saying good-bye to the Funks, we saddled up, pointed 'em east, and hit the trail. After almost 750 miles of Big Sky country, we expected to be leaving it behind as we would soon cross the state line into North Dakota. With almost 1,400 miles behind us, we would be nearing the halfway point of our trip in a few days. This would also be the point where Dale headed north and we would trek a little south. After riding together for almost two weeks, I knew it would be hard to say adios, but we still had a few days before that happened, and we'd already decided on a night out in Minot, North Dakota, before we parted ways.

MONTANA WAS A mighty big state, and the diversity it offered was incredible. It offered everything from breathtaking mountains and streams, mountain goats and grizzly bears, to wide open spaces and unbelievable winds. And I guess it decided to hold onto us for one more day. In reality, I'm not sure if Montana was holding onto us or if we were just reluctant to let go. There is a song with the lyrics "Should I stay or should I go now?" and that is how we often felt on our trip. We experienced beautiful areas with wonderful people, often creating in us reluctance to move on. At the same time, we knew that more of the same was down the road and, consequently, this bike trip once again mimicked life as we struggled to find a balance of the past, present, and future.

Leaving Wolf Point at 1:00 P.M. and staying on Highway 2, we decided on a relatively short day of 56 miles. Despite the late start, our friendly jet stream grabbed us by the seat of our pants and blew us into Culbertson in a little over two hours. I couldn't imagine doing this trip from east to west against the prevailing winds. More power to those who choose that route, but just like I loved the thrill of riding down the mountains versus the work of climbing them, I would also embrace incredible tailwinds versus headwinds any day. I had to chuckle when I thought of a woman who attended a slide show I did about my previous Florida-to-Wisconsin bike trip: After describing how we flew south to Florida and then biked north back to Wisconsin, she posed the question, "Why didn't you start in Wisconsin so you could ride downhill to Florida instead of uphill to Wisconsin?" At the time, I was not quite sure how to respond, thinking she was jerking my chain and not serious. No matter what the direction, I would take downhill with a tailwind every time.

WE HAD PLANNED to bike to Williston, North Dakota, that day. Because it was only about 40 miles away, we dilly-dallied in Culbertson that morning, grabbing breakfast at a diner where we met another bicyclist, Bob. Biker Bob was traveling alone from Michigan, and was heading to Los Angeles. With a smile and a handshake he offered tips on roads to come. His bike squeaked and his clothes were tattered, and as we parted ways, we saw he was biking with radio earphones plugged in. Biking in the same direction as traffic, and in his case, into strong headwinds, he would have difficulty hearing traffic approach from behind, even without music. We wished Biker Bob well, and headed for different coastlines. Two days later we were shocked to hear that a car had hit and killed Bob west of Glasgow, Montana. Despite our brief interaction with him, we found Bob to be a kindred spirit, and we could not help but feel his loss and also recognize our vulnerability to the thousands of vehicles that passed by in the course of our trip.

We left Culbertson around 4:30 P.M., and realized we would pay the piper again. North Dakota greeted us with a 25 MPH southeast headwind as well as a good dose of hills, as if to mock our comments about the flatlands. To add to this, I was cursed for the second time with the *ping* of a broken spoke. This time, I was not so lucky, as the broken spoke was on the freewheel side of the wheel, necessitating removal of the gear cluster for repair. With my tools out, I also realized that the head of my freewheel tool was too large for my adjustable wrench. Unfortunately, Dale's wrench wouldn't open wide enough either. Sitting on Highway 2 late in the afternoon with the wind in my face, things did not look good. Fortunately, God takes care of fools, even fools with the wrong tools.

Looking off to the north I saw an oil well crew working around a rig out on the open plains. I initially thought that Denise would likely have the best chance to charm these roughnecks into lending us a wrench, but then I also realized that aspect of the plan could backfire for the same reasons. Sucking it up, I took it upon myself to hike up to the rig, the whole time attempting to look as tough as a guy can look when borrowing a tool wearing bike shorts and shoes. Approaching these guys, I felt a little bit like Custer must have felt over a hundred years ago as he rode out into these open plains anticipating a less-than-welcome reception. In this case, all that was shot in my direction were a few raised eyebrows and a couple of snickers as they handed me an adjustable wrench more suited to turning the nuts of a bulldozer. In short order, the gear cluster was off, the spoke was changed, the wrench was timidly returned, and we were back in the saddle.

We rolled into Williston at 9:30 P.M., with just enough time to use our last gift certificates at McDonald's. At 10 P.M., we made camp between two buildings on a college campus. As we finally crawled into our bags to end a very long, challenging day, I felt for the first time in our trip that my attitude had taken a downturn.

THE NEXT MORNING, I awoke with the same bad attitude I had gone to sleep with—no way to start a new day. This was no doubt due to being a little worn out, having mechanical problems, and the bad news about Biker Bob.

Williston was a fairly busy, dusty city full of young guys working the oil rig industry. Williston was not a bad place, but it was easy to see that the upswing in the oil business brought a lot of temporary workers into the area. For these workers, mostly young guys with no family or roots in town, this was an opportunity to work hard and play hard. As visitors ourselves, we certainly didn't have any roots there and definitely weren't leaving much money behind, so I couldn't blame the community for catering to the oil boom. It was just not a scene that fit with what our trip had been thus far. Bicycles and oil booms were not a good match.

I realized I needed to turn myself around. I was in one of those funks where I'd probably complain if my executioner wanted to hang me with a new rope. Taking only enough time in Williston to grab a donut at a bakery, stop at a gas station to grind down my freewheel tool to fit my wrench (much appreciated), and mail home some unneeded gear, we headed out of town as soon as possible. Three miles out of town, we encountered a road construction crew working on a road with no pavement, and a water-spraying truck whose driver thought it would be cute to spray us (real cute!). About this time, Denise crashed into the mud and, although unhurt, was quite a sight. Her worst injury was from having to endure her new nickname of "Cow Patty."

Along this stretch, we bumped into four other bikers on a long tour and realized in short order that we needed to avoid them. A few folks had mentioned a group of bikers ahead of us who weren't exactly establishing a great reputation for other cyclists. As the stories went, they were rude, drank a lot, and had been kicked out of one camping area. After spending just a short time visiting with them, we saw that their reputation resembled them. They were loud, boisterous know-it-alls who seemed to think we would be interested in their shenanigans. As they laughed and bragged about being tossed from the campsite, we were glad to hear that our paths ahead were divergent. They were headed for Florida, and we were glad to see them turn south.

Seventy-five miles down Highway 2, we hit the town of Stanley, and found a nice park, free hot showers, and an open market next door. After a day of bad attitude, I was certain this would be just the ticket to turn things around.

CHAPTER 7

Parting Ways—
On Our Way

IN THE SPAN of 24 hours, we had experienced the yin and the yang of North Dakota. Whereas Williston had been congested, dusty, and loud, Stanley was airy, clean, and peaceful. A beautiful park with free camping and hot showers, and I felt like a new bike right off the showroom floor. Departing Stanley that following morning, we knew we would have a relatively short (60-mile) day to Minot, North Dakota. Minot was the largest town we would hit since starting out in Vancouver, British Columbia, and it would also be where we'd part company with Dale. A plan for a night out on the town before splitting up was brewing, but our options seemed fairly limited due to funds. We also felt challenged by our need to find a safe place to store our gear, and how we'd get around with only bikes as our transportation.

Riding into Minot on a busy four-lane road, I had dropped about a quarter-mile behind Denise and Dale when a guy riding a bike the opposite direction swung a loop around and yelled for me to hold up. Kim Hocking was a nursing student at a university in Minot. Seeing us with our bikes and gear, he wondered if we had any tips for a two-week bike trip he had planned. Catching me a bit by surprise, and before I could offer any immediate suggestions or thoughts, Kim shifted gears.

"Do you guys have a place to stay tonight?" Knowing opportunity when I saw it, I replied, "Not yet, but we were hoping to find a place for the night where we could hit the town a little."

I recognize it might be unfair to imply that all college students know where and how to party, but it turned out that Kim fit that generalization.

Denise and Dale had looped back to find me, and we followed Kim back to campus, where he lined up dorm rooms to bunk in, and a full itinerary for the evening.

We spent the evening telling Kim stories of our trip, answering questions, and offering advice for his upcoming trip. We filled him in with a myriad of useful tidbits such as bringing a good ground cloth, a comfortable sleeping pad, and spare tubes. I stressed my thoughts about keeping a good journal and keeping the journey the focus and not the end point. When Denise left for a few minutes I gave him the really important lowdown, "No matter how good someone makes it sound, don't let them talk you into taking a day off to go for a side trip on horseback!"

With evening approaching, it was time to hit the town for some quiet music, pizza, and a couple beers. Kim had other plans!

We began our celebration at an outdoor picnic/pre-wedding party with champagne. As the sun went down, all of us were just lighting up. With Kim as our designated driver, Denise rode shotgun in Kim's Datsun truck and Dale and I rode in the open back singing, "We come from Montana, we wear a bandana, our spurs are of silver, our ponies are gray." We drove to a bar called the Fireside or something similar. After Kim shared our cross-continent biker's story with the bouncers, who waived the cover charge for us, we were out on the crowded dance floor. The fact that none of us could dance whatsoever didn't slow us down, and the champagne mixed with beer certainly didn't lend to inhibitions for any of us.

The night at the Fireside ended when one of the band members thought his girlfriend was spending too much time on the dance floor around me (how was I to know?). Some gal set her sights on Dale, and he was ready to escape. Like so many nights when we know it's an obvious time to head home, we instead chose another fork in the road and decided 1:30 A.M. was the perfect time for pizza and a last beer. I don't recall if the pizza was good, although I ate a lot of it. When Kim dropped a tray with a full pitcher of beer and four glasses on the floor, we realized 2:30 A.M. was a good time to call it a night.

WE AWOKE IN the morning wishing we could have a "do-over." Strong black coffee was definitely the first order of the day. Though we all looked like we were at a casting call for

Night of the Living Dead, we had to admit that it had been one heck of a night out.

Kim left for other obligations, and Denise and I knew the time had come to part company with Dale. Ten days of riding together might not sound like much, but this had been a special ten days in our lives. We shared the experience of fulfilling our dreams in that ten days. Riding together had enhanced each of our own trips and had created a special, unexpected trip segment that none of us could have planned.

As often occurs in partings of this nature, we made plans and promises to see one another again, knowing full well it may never come to pass. We knew that when such encounters and adventures end, despite best intentions, life always seemed to have a way of tucking us back inside envelopes or catching us up in day-to-day existence. For the moment, though, we said the words, exchanged hugs and handshakes, and rolled onward toward the Atlantic Ocean on separate paths. Whether or not we would truly see each other again, I knew Dale would be permanently etched into my memory. A tall, dark, thin guy with a mile-wide smile, he was living a dream while raising money for Special Olympics. Denise and I both wished Dale bright skies, a safe trip, and plentiful tailwinds.

AFTER OVER 750 miles on Highway 2, Denise and I headed out of Minot in a southeasterly direction on Highway 52. The wind gods continued to smile on us with a great tailwind. Despite a late start at 11:00 A.M., we knocked off 95 miles, blowing through the tiny towns of Balfour and Anamoose before stopping in Harvey. Denise had not been feeling up to par, and we decided she should see a doctor at a local clinic in Harvey. A doctor—who just happened to stop in the office on his way fishing (donned in a hat with flies attached)—ran a few tests and determined Denise had an infection. With medication in hand, we continued on.

Just down the road from Harvey, we stopped for the night in the town of Fessenden. Once again, we couldn't believe our luck as we pulled into a free campground with a town swimming pool. With a refreshing swim and a quick meal—due to ravenous mosquitoes—we called it a day, realizing that the following day would be our last in North Dakota.

Drawing near to our home states of Minnesota and Wisconsin felt a bit strange. How would we feel when we entered Wisconsin, and then biked over the same routes that had been training rides for our trip? We looked forward to seeing friends and family in my hometown of Oshkosh, Wisconsin, on our way east, and to refueling on home-cooked meals. Would it be difficult to then leave again after a brief layover?

AFTER A GREAT breakfast the following morning, we hit the trail out of Fessenden by 10 A.M. With the wind at our backs, we decided to shoot for Valley City about 118 miles away. Highway 52 ended at its junction with Interstate 94 in Jamestown, and we decided to ride the interstate to Valley City and then into Minnesota the following day.

It's funny how the familiarity of I-94 almost felt inviting and welcoming. Before this trip, if someone had told me we would bike 65 miles on I-94, I would have said they were crazy. Undoubtedly some would question the sanity of taking an interstate highway on bicycle and, in fact, it is illegal to do so in some states, such as Wisconsin. But when we considered our options, we realized that although it was a four-lane interstate, it was not that heavily traveled. Although we had loved our time in the mountains and valleys and most definitely enjoyed the roads that kept us in touch with the people and places we passed, on a trip of such nature, you do what works. We certainly looked forward to leaving the interstate and its downsides—the scenery kind of sucked and the noise was a pain—but traveling the interstate fulfilled the purpose of getting us quickly and directly from point A to point B. Most importantly, it had an eight-foot paved shoulder that provided us with the widest buffer we'd had between us and traffic on the entire trip. Riding on this grey ribbon of super slab reminded me of our time early in the trip as we forged our way through the quagmire of the Hope Slide in British Columbia. Although significantly different from each other, they each challenged us. Neither of these routes would constitute our first choice of travel conditions, but in both cases we kept the pedals spinning and the miles passing. Sometimes that was the best you could hope for.

Although a rather uneventful day, we did put in 118 miles, making for one of the longer mileage days of our trip. The following day, we would enter Minnesota, the Land of 10,000 Lakes. After a thousand miles of open plains, the thought of lakes, trees, and roads with curves was a pleasant anticipation.

WITH ABOUT 40 miles of I-94 stretching east ahead of us, we hit the highway for Minnesota the following morning. Part of our reason for this direct ride on I-94 was that, despite the medication, Denise was still not feeling all that great. On this route, we would be able to stop at my aunt and uncle's place in Fridley, Minnesota. We could also see another doctor there, if necessary. I'd learned it takes a lot for Denise to be slowed down and even more for her to complain, so I knew I was really going to have to make sure she didn't push herself too hard.

I struggled as we crossed North Dakota and it became easy to lay blame on the state for my struggles. But the conflicts I dealt with lay within me. My frustrations with bike issues, the occasional inconsiderate driver and Denise's health issues made it easy to make North Dakota my scapegoat. The reality was that North Dakota, in my case, found itself sandwiched between the excitement and exhilaration present at the start of our trip, and the anticipation of biking into our home "stomping grounds." Biking in the rain in Vancouver for the first three days of our trip was not pleasant, but having occurred during the "honeymoon" of our journey certainly made it easier to forgive the transgression. By the time we reached North Dakota the trip and I were like an old married couple, at times too quick to poke at each other for minor indiscretions.

I realized my perceptions of North Dakota were conflicted. Although the state is geographically flat, I found myself on a daily roller coaster of emotions that required mentally shifting gears to adjust to the transitions we encountered. The contrasts were stark and abrupt. One oil crew was kind enough to lend us a wrench, yet the next crew sped by in their pick-up trucks within inches of us, enveloping us in clouds of dust. One day we rode incredible tailwinds, only to face its evil twin, headwinds the next. Williston did not appear to have the time or place for bicyclists, but in Stanley just down the road we felt very welcome.

The people of North Dakota were a rugged, no-nonsense type that I liked and appreciated. North Dakota can be a harsh state; a living isn't just handed out, but rather has to be extracted through hard work and perseverance. The earliest settlers in this area had to be tough or they didn't survive, and these attributes had no doubt been passed down through the generations. Although the times and circumstances have perhaps changed, survival in North Dakota still requires a breed of folks who know hard work and tough times.

Having cycled through some of America's most pristine areas in Idaho and Montana and anticipating the forests and lake areas of Minnesota and Wisconsin, I was holding North Dakota to unfair standards. Apples and oranges are different but neither is better than the other. I had to look deeper within myself to find the beauty of North Dakota, and when I did, I found in fact, the contrasts and starkness are its beauty.

CHAPTER 8

Home Roads

"WELCOME TO MINNESOTA" beckoned us from just across the Red River. Just prior to entering the bridge a sharp *ping* penetrated the morning air as the by now all too familiar sound of a breaking spoke reached my ears. Limping to a stop I broke out my tools as a stranger walked up. Dan stopped to chat and lend a hand and soon I was back on the road. Just as one settler might have helped a stranger with a broken wagon wheel a hundred years ago, North Dakotans were still helping strangers with wheels in 1981. With a fresh spoke and a refreshed attitude thanks to Dan, we rolled into Minnesota, the fifth state of our trip. Already the scenery had changed to one of woods and lakes as we traveled southeasterly on Highway 10 headed for Detroit Lakes.

Pulling up in Detroit Lakes was a bit of a shock to our systems. We had been anxious to leave behind the broad open prairies with their sparse sprinkling of people, but here we hit a town packed with people for Aquafest, the area's largest celebration of the summer. Traffic and people were everywhere, but the lively action of cars, boats, and teenagers being teenagers was about enough to make us retreat back west. Not only was the Legion Campground full, but it was also busy and loud. We decided to escape the crowd and head out of town. Rolling out of town, we slowed down as a car began backing out of a driveway in front of us. While the car's driver waited for a lull in traffic and we neared, the woman in the passenger seat rolled down her window and asked where we were headed. Tired, I gave the short version of our trip and our camping dilemma for the evening. As the road cleared, she offered, "We're running late but you're welcome to set up your tent out back; garage is open and there are cold drinks in the old fridge." With that, they were on their way. We took them up on their offer to camp in the backyard, and with an ice-cold pop, we settled in for the night after another 113-mile day.

At this point in our trip and after experiencing the kindness of so many strangers, we probably shouldn't have been surprised with this latest generosity, but we were. In the span of a minute, these folks whose names we didn't even get gave us a safe place to make camp, as well as much appreciated cold drinks. Sawing logs before they returned and on the road before they were up, we never did exchange any more information with each other. This lack of information actually made the experience more valuable to us, knowing that strangers still extend trust and kindness based solely on the briefest of encounters.

DESPITE SEVERAL 100-PLUS-MILE days strung together, we both felt pretty good the following morning, starting early at 7:00 A.M. With the exception of Denise's ailment, we felt pretty strong from a month's worth of riding. Any extra pounds had disappeared, and our bodies had become efficient at cranking out the miles.

The demands on the body were great as we fought to stay ahead on calorie intake. It's one thing to train for and complete a single century (100-mile) ride, but it was an altogether different thing to string together 30 of them in a row. Often we would consume in a single day the number of calories we would otherwise take in over three days. Burgers, soup, fries, malts, salads, fruit, anything and everything when available, went into the furnace and came out in the form of leg rotations on pedals at about 80 times per minute, or approximately 40,000 rotations a day. We continued to lose weight on this trip, simply because our calorie intake was often less than our energy output. Sometimes the deficient calorie intake was due to lack of funds; other times it was from lack of food availability; still other times, we were just too tired to put in the effort to cook at the end of the day. More money would have meant more food, but we were fine as we were. Thanks to the many invitations into people's homes, we often ate like royalty.

That morning, we clipped off the first 70 miles like nothing, and rolled into Staples, Minnesota. Here, Railroad Days was in full swing and for $1.00, we dug into a big hot turkey sandwich, baked beans, coleslaw, chips, and lemonade. It was such a good deal, I had to have it twice—and it was just as tasty the second time around. It was impossible to eat too much, but I also realized that it would be a whole different story when the trip ended. I could become Bob the Balloon if I didn't shift gears back to normal eating habits.

Spying our bikes and gear, a reveler named Allen approached and began asking questions. His inquiries about our trip soon turned to criticism. He was one of those know-it-all, done-it-all types—a "bride at every wedding" and a "corpse at every funeral." According to him, we couldn't have come the way we had and we needed to change the way we were going. Quite honestly, I think the guy had a spoke loose upstairs. One second he was critical of the route we were riding, and the next he was ranting about something that had nothing to do with us. When he asked me why I didn't shave my legs like most serious bikers, I knew it was time to say "adios, buddy!" He reminded me of the old joke about wrestling with a pig: After a while, you realize that you're getting dirty and the pig is having fun. I guess experiences wouldn't be unique without unique people.

After refueling, we headed off again, and hit Little Falls, Minnesota, by the end of our day. We had planned to look up Denise's close friend, Julie, but it turned out that she was out of town. When we pulled into Lindbergh State Park, we were a bit put off by the $5.00 camping fee, but we couldn't resist the hot showers. We had covered another 103 miles, and we were definitely getting into familiar country.

At this point, we had certainly transitioned into an area with a much more dense population, with towns and communities often just miles from one another. We expected this as we approached Minneapolis, but even when expected, it was another adjustment for us. We were traveling Highway 10, and although it had a wide, paved shoulder, we found ourselves engulfed in noise, exhaust, and heavy traffic that put us on edge. We could have easily adjusted our route to bypass the Twin Cities, but we wanted to ride through these familiar areas and visit with friends and relatives along the way. We planned to stop over in River Falls, Wisconsin, just across the St. Croix River from Minnesota, to visit with friends and do some serious overhaul work on our bikes before heading to the East Coast.

Denise was looking a little wobbly on her bike, and she had developed a rash. She was not complaining, but she intended to see a doctor when we stopped for the night at my aunt and uncle's home.

We had traveled 65 miles thus far for the day, and kept plugging along with the traffic, until Denise yelled out, "Stop! I've got a flat."

Looping back, I could see from her body language that she was struggling. We made the repair as quickly as possible. It was now afternoon, and we were back amid the increasing traffic. A short distance down the road, we heard a loud *bang*. A car that had just passed us limped to the shoulder. The woman driving stepped out of the car with a bewildered look on her face. We rolled up, and she pointed back into the roadway to a muffler exhaust pipe she had just run over.

"I didn't even have a chance to swerve. All of a sudden it was just there. I hit it, and now look," as she pointed to her flat front tire.

With traffic continued to fly by, and the woman quite obviously in need of help, I suggested, "Why don't you pull it over more, pop your trunk, and I'll take care of it."

As the woman went to do so, I heard a loud yelp from Denise. With the intention of pulling the offending muffler off the road before it claimed another victim, she had gone out onto the road. Too late she realized that the muffler had just recently fallen off a passing car and was still hotter than the bottom step of hell. As I stood on a busy highway with a lady and her flat tire, and a partner with an infection, a rash, and now a burn, things seemed a bit bleak. Fortunately, Denise's burn was minor, and we were able to change the tire fairly quickly. The woman was very appreciative, and we felt good about being able to repay some of the kindness that we had been shown. Soon we were all on our way once more.

We had 30 miles to go in heavy traffic before we could stop, so we forged ahead. Fifteen miles later, I heard, "***t, ***t, ***t," from Denise. I knew this wasn't going to be good: Denise was usually not one to cuss. I turned to see her stopped on the shoulder, head down looking at yet another flat, and I knew this day had to end soon.

I pulled out our tools as Denise sat on the roadside. The exhaust of a hundred passing cars wafted around us, the daylight faded, and we repaired the third flat tire of the day (two bikes, one car). Fortunately, we were soon back on the road and arrived at my relatives' house in Fridley by 8:30 P.M. With tired bodies, frayed nerves, and ravenous appetites, we sat down to a wonderful dinner. In the warm home of my aunt and uncle, Lorraine and Skip Gams, the past day's miles once again melted away, the embrace of family replacing the day's difficulties. After visiting a while, we called it a night; our sleeping bags rolled out on a carpeted living room floor.

WE TOOK ADVANTAGE of being in a community where Denise could see a doctor. The rash she had developed had been really miserable for her, and though she was a tough girl, there was no way she could continue to bike without some help. Fortunately, she received a quick diagnosis. The medication the doctor in North Dakota had prescribed necessitated not exposing herself to direct sunlight—something he neglected to tell her, despite the fact that she told him we were on a cross-country bicycle trip. We had appreciated the fact that he had seen her that morning in Harvey when he had not been on duty, but I think he must have been thinking more about trout than Denise's well-being that morning. With new medications in hand, and $53.00 out of our funds, we continued on.

My cousin Paul Gams had decided to bike with us for a while. Five miles down the road, you guessed it: Paul flatted. The traffic had been building and none of us had supplies to fix his tube, so Paul insisted we keep going and that he would find a way home. We wished him luck, and with feelings of guilt, we abandoned him and continued on.

We looked forward to crossing into Wisconsin as we exited Fridley on Highway 96. We rolled into Stillwater, Minnesota, a quaint small town directly across from Wisconsin on the St. Croix River, riding the front winds of a heavy rainstorm.

To get out of the rain, we ducked into Brine's Meat Market on Stillwater's main drag. Previously we had biked to Stillwater several times on training rides from River Falls, Wisconsin, and a stop at Brine's for a small lunch had always been a treat when we could spare the money. Stopping at Brine's was just the first of what would be familiar stops in the week ahead as we traveled the roads of our old haunts.

With a break from the rain, hot soup in our bellies, and Wisconsin calling loudly from across the St. Croix River, we rolled over the historic old lift bridge and crossed into my home state. Immediately greeted by a large wooden "Welcome to Wisconsin" sign, we pulled up, intent on snapping a picture of this milestone. Walking my bike up to the sign, the odometer that I had set at the start in Vancouver hit exactly 2,000 miles—on the head, to the tenth of a mile. Significantly, this marked the approximate halfway point of our trip. Being July 20th, it also marked the one-month anniversary of being on the road. The places we'd seen and the people we'd met were more valuable than money in the bank. Dealing with the adversity of equipment failures, adjusting to unpredictable weather conditions, and perhaps most importantly, dealing with a broad diversity of people and their related issues would undoubtedly be valuable in post–bike trip life. I remembered the question put to me repeatedly prior to starting out: "How can you afford to take the summer off and not earn money for school?" I now knew without a doubt that my answer—"How can I afford not to?"—had been as true as a perfect wheel. There would be plenty of a time to earn money, but opportunities like this trip would be hard to come by. What lay ahead was still anybody's guess, but with these miles of experience under our belt, we both felt better equipped to deal with whatever we encountered. Following a brief photo shoot, we hopped back on our bikes.

When we pulled into River Falls, Wisconsin, after a 50-mile day, the whole experience felt a bit surreal. Prior to starting out, our time was spent on the stuff of mundane day-to-day life. Now, there were surprises around every bend and over every hill. When we walked in the door of Tim Paterick's Village Pedaler, we were treated a little bit like local heroes. Tim had been a tremendous help to us throughout the past year. Both Denise and I had bought our bikes from Tim: I bought a copper-orange 12-speed, and Denise picked out a bronze Trek made in Wisconsin. There was nothing like that feeling of coming home.

The questions flew fast and furious:

"What's been the toughest part so far?"

"Any close calls?"

"Are the bikes holding up?"

"Are you holding up?"

With the continued barrage, we took the opportunity to work on bike tune-ups as we regaled our friends with stories of bear attacks (in my mind), gypsies (which were real), and flat tires (of which we had our share). It was so good to be with our friends.

After several hours, we had to say our good-byes. Like everyone we met along the way, these friends were intrigued and interested in our trip and often expressed a wish that they could do the same. The reality, however, was that the folks we met along the way, although helpful and interested, had busy lives that offered limited time away from the requirements of jobs, families, and life in general. And such was the case with Tim and his shop crew, as they had to get on with the day's demands.

We exchanged hugs and handshakes, promising them the full story and a slideshow at the end of summer when we returned for fall semester, and moved on. Riding past the university, I contemplated my approaching last year of college, along with student teaching as a vocational agriculture instructor. I tried to imagine how we would feel when this trip was over and we were back on the ride of everyday life. Would it be boring?

Rolling through the familiar countryside of our pre-trip training rides, I remembered the eager anticipation Denise and I felt. Anxious to travel new roads and meet new people we had looked forward to whatever awaited us. The 2,000 miles that stretched out behind us had been challenging and new, however, these familiar roads that had become "old hat" during our preparations now rose up to meet us and welcome us home. I'd come to realize that one doesn't have to travel around the world to experience new and different places and people. A world of diversity exists within our own fifty states and even within the borders of any individual state. I would suggest, however, finding a way to branch out from the beaten path of interstate highways and large cities, and creating accessibility to people along the way. For us, slowing the pace via nonmotorized travel opened doors to the places we passed through and the people we met. If we had been on a motorcycle even, people we met may have felt an intimidation factor that would have kept us at arm's length. This is not to say that there's anything wrong with that mode of travel; we probably would have experienced a similar intimacy traveling via canoe or sailboat versus a powerboat. Perhaps this is due to a perceived vulnerability of a human-powered, quiet form of travel that encourages folks to not only come forward to meet us but also to open their homes to us.

As we biked out of town, we headed for our friends Clark and Sue's house, where we planned to spend the night. Only as we began to climb a very steep and long hill out of "Happy Valley Road" did I remember from training rides that the "happy" part was only experienced when heading downhill back to town. Thirty minutes later, we arrived to share a wonderful meal with good friends.

Clark Garry, a good friend of mine, was a biology professor at the University of Wisconsin, River Falls. We shared a passion for cross-country skiing and, through his mentoring, I became a much better skier. Clark and his wife Sue always had some adventure cooking in their lives, and we spent a great evening sharing "tales of the road."

Saying good-bye to the Garrys the next morning, we once again hit the road. With half of our trip behind us, we felt a bit validated in our endeavor. I'd guess some people thought we'd never make it, and perhaps at times, I myself wondered. But like a freight train with the weight of box cars making stopping difficult, we felt propelled down the road by the 2,000 miles behind us. Like that train though, we knew we'd have trouble stopping when the time came.

WITH A SOLID night's rest from staying at the home of friends, I was fired up to start this leg of the trip. Unfortunately, Denise was struggling to overcome the dermatitis she developed from medication she received in North Dakota. The pills for the rash had their own side effect, making her extremely drowsy, but she said she was good to go. More than once on this trip, I'd realized Denise's strength, particularly when the chips were down. The trip would have been a completely different thing had she been one of those people who constantly complained, never did her share of the work, and worst of all, brought an attitude that pulled others down. Denise was just the opposite, and I couldn't have imagined a better partner.

Leaving River Falls behind, we traveled southeasterly heading for Ellsworth, Wisconsin, where we would pick up Highway 10. I could see that, despite Denise's best efforts and no complaints, she was just not up for the day. We decided to make it a short, 25-mile day and made camp at a wayside rest area. What Denise needed more than anything were just a few days off to really rest and get things cleared up.

My folks' house in Oshkosh, Wisconsin, was only a couple of days away. We agreed to make that a rest stop for two or three days, seeing how she felt by then. Denise was already sound asleep at 4:00 P.M., so I took some time with my journal and a book. My quiet time was interrupted by a car pulling up and the sound of garbage cans being tipped over. Looking out of the tent, I prepared myself to deal with some kids raising hell, but instead, saw an elderly couple pulling aluminum cans out of the garbage. Hoping they didn't have to do this just to make ends meet, it reminded me of how blessed I was to have good career opportunities down the road.

While a light rain pattered on the tent fly, the folks outside cleaned up the garbage and drove off. Inside, I contemplated the next day's ride. I hoped Denise would feel better. If not, I would call my brother Jim to pick her up and take her to Oshkosh for some extra rest time.

I KNEW HIGHWAY 10 would be a direct route across Wisconsin, and the traffic on the two-lane road was not usually that bad because most people stayed on Interstate 94. This route followed our spring training ride from River Falls to Oshkosh, the same one where we had the misfortune of having our money stolen in Plum City. With that in mind, we made the none-to-difficult decision to bypass Plum City, trekking eastward through scenic countryside of rolling hills, curves, and forestland. After our time in the mountains, these hills that once seemed huge were now insignificant.

Keeping an eye on Denise, I could see she was struggling and even wobbling a bit as she tried to put on a good show. Moving slowly down the highway and even weaving slightly was certainly not normal for her, nor was it safe. "How do you feel today?" I asked, knowing the response I'd get.

"I'm doing all right, just a bit tired."

I'd been in her shoes before, and I knew it was no fun when every revolution of the pedals was a chore and staying awake was hard.

No matter how much she kept up the charade, I knew better and pushed the issue. "You know, we've got almost 2,000 miles ahead of us, and right now would be the perfect time for us to pull a little rest time."

Receiving an edgy reply of, "I'll be okay," I knew this was not going to be easy.

"If you catch a ride to Oshkosh with Jim, you'll only be riding over miles you already biked this year, so it's not like you didn't bike across the country this summer."

She gave me a skeptical look that seemed to ask, "Would that work for you?" and I thought I detected a slight waiver in her resolve.

"Look, it's just one day of riding, and if we make it a three-day layover, you'll be done with your meds and good to go. If you don't take this break, I think you might get so rundown that it might be the end of this trip. If you don't finish, I don't finish."

I could see the resignation on her face as we coasted to a stop. Much as she wanted to tough it out, she knew the right decision was to grab the ride and get the rest. We stopped at a gas station, where I was able to reach my brother Jim. Fortunately, he and his girlfriend Jan were able to drive to meet us.

We agreed to continue on until we met them, and it was easy to see we had made the right decision as I watched Denise grapple with the road. Two hours later, just west of Neillsville, we saw Jim and Jan pull up to the rescue in front of a grocery store in a red Duster. By this point in the day, we had already covered over 90 miles, and I knew by the look on Denise's face that she had reached her limit. It was unbelievable she had put in those kind of miles, but I knew she had needed to show me that she could.

We loaded her gear and her into the car, said our goodbyes, and although I'd only be alone for the night and next day, I had a twinge in my gut as I waved and they headed east. This was definitely the right decision, but nonetheless, a difficult one for both of us. We had just biked 2,000 miles and spent every minute together for the last month as we crossed the country. Feeling pretty alone as the car disappeared from sight, I wondered how long it would be before she was sound asleep. I hoped my optimism for her to recover was not unfounded.

Getting back in the pedals, I focused on my own needs of finding a camping spot for the night. Spying a church just off the road, I approached the pastor who was outside doing grounds work. I introduced myself, described our trip, and asked if I could set up my tent for the night, explaining that I'd be on the road early the next morning. I was a bit surprised when his response indicated to me that he had never bought into the parts of the Bible about making welcome the weary traveler. Realizing I probably looked a little rough around the edges, I thanked him anyway. Continuing on, I felt more than a little sorry for myself—without my partner and having been rejected by one of God's front men.

Fortunately, just as things were looking fairly bleak, a ray of sunshine broke through in the form of Jim Buttersworth, a recent graduate of UW–River Falls and now a PCA (Production Credit Association) employee. It was only through good luck that Jim had pulled up alongside me in his car and recognized me from classes we shared while attending UW–River Falls. Aside from those classes, Jim and I shared the acquaintance of Steve Katner, my partner on the Florida trip the previous summer. Jim had also heard about our cross-country trip from speaking with Steve, who was going to be joining Denise and me on the remainder of our trip from Oshkosh to Maine.

Over hot pizza, cold beer, and a promise of a roof over my head, I told Jim stories about the trip. Back at his house, I closed my eyes and drifted off to sleep, my last thought an apology to the Lord for feeling a little put out earlier when I was turned away at the church. He just had a better deal waiting for me down the road.

MY PLAN WAS to make it to Oshkosh that next day, so I knew an early start was necessary. With a quick, light breakfast, I was on the road at 6:30 A.M. Riding alone, I realized that riding with a partner made the journey much more enjoyable. I thought about riding with Dale Reiber through parts of Montana and North Dakota for ten days, and wondered about his thoughts on riding with people versus riding solo. For me, the best times were those Denise and I had shared; even the difficult times were easier with the support from each other. I realized that some enjoy the "lone wolf" approach, but me, I guess I'm a bit in the "herd" mentality. To each his own.

Before Denise had caught a ride with Jim and Jan to Oshkosh the previous day, we had crossed over Interstate 94 and looked over at a pine plantation to the north. This was where we had camped on our training ride to Oshkosh the previous spring, when our money had been stolen. That evening, we had just enough money left to share one meal at a truck stop across the road from this same pine plantation, and for the following two days, literally all we had eaten until reaching Oshkosh had been bread and water. Somehow that hadn't seemed that bad as we settled into our tent tucked in the pines. It was funny to reflect back on that night, when we had spent the evening envisioning how this trip would be. At that time, we could never have guessed the turns our trip would take. The very fact that I was riding alone today spoke volumes on the issue of the need to adapt.

With Denise in Oshkosh recuperating, I was riding alone for the first time in over 2,000 miles. I knew that it was going to be a long day as I put down my head and spun the pedals. Without stopping once, not even getting caught by a red light or stop sign, I put on 85 miles before I put a foot on the ground and stopped for some lunch in Waupaca. Throughout the ride that day, I rolled past memories of growing up in that area. At the time, I had written in my journal about how so much had changed in the area since I was a young kid, and I had wondered how much things would change in the future.

With miles to go before I slept, and my butt definitely sore from the long stint in the saddle that morning, I jumped back on before it became too hard to do so. A light mist turned into a steady rain as I reached the town of Freemont. With the weather reminding me of our first days in Vancouver, I pulled up in front of a local cheese factory store, feeling tired and damp. Over the years, the store had been a favorite of mine for fresh cheese curds and Limburger cheese, also known as "stink cheese." And because the day's weather truly stunk, my cheese choice was easy. With a quarter pound of Limburger in hand, I headed next door to an old brick-front bar. Only in Wisconsin could you walk into a bar with Limburger cheese, pull up a stool, order a cold one, and share this aromatic treat with a couple of old guys who actually appreciated it. When my newfound friends heard about "the trip," they had a ton of questions and comments. An hour went by way too fast and the bar stool felt way better than my bike seat, so it was with some reluctance that I pushed away from the bar. Bidding my new buddies farewell, I hit the road, no doubt leaving a mile-long scent trail behind me. With a couple of beers and some of Wisconsin's finest stoking my body, I knocked off the final miles of a long, 133-mile day. I had 2,300 miles behind me as I rolled the last 30 miles toward Oshkosh, lost in thoughts about previous bicycle escapades that paved the way for this current adventure.

CHAPTER 9

Paving the Way

IDENTIFYING EXACTLY WHICH events in our lives lead us to where we currently find ourselves is often difficult. Nearing Oshkosh, my thoughts circled around three previous bike trips. The first took place near our family home, located on the west shore of Lake Winnebago, about halfway between Oshkosh and Neenah. With the lake to our east and farm fields to the west, our neighborhood consisted of a single strip of homes belonging to average blue-collar families. Like many kids who grew up in the 1950s and 1960s, our neighborhood still consisted of neighbors, meaning it was still a time when families' lives were intertwined as they grew through good and bad times. Parents counted on one another to look out for the kids, and in our neighborhood, it was tough to get away with anything with neighbors like Erna Selwitchka or Frances Karow keeping an eye on us.

For kids in the early 1960s, bikes had been, hands down, our most valuable possessions. Riding with training wheels was about a one-day orientation before we graduated to two-wheelers—gladly accepting the inevitable road rash, proudly wearing the scabs and scrapes to our knees and elbows.

Just like this cross-continent trip of exploration filled me with the excitement of new places and people, the same feeling had embraced my friend Rob and me in 1962, as we had contemplated a trip on our own to the Carp Pond, made possible with the new freedom of our bikes. The Carp Pond was basically a holding pond for rough fish, and was about a 3½-mile one-way trip by bike. For two 7-year-olds who were not supposed to go any farther than our beach road, this trip had involved all the unknowns and mysterious intrigue of a 4,000-mile cross-country trip.

Typically we kids were left to our own adventures between breakfast and supper, and we figured our best chance to make a break for it would be mid-morning. At that time, our dads would be at work, our moms busy with household chores, and our sisters, who would squeal on us for sure if they knew what we were up to, would be busy doing girl stuff. Plotting our journey the day before, we had pooled our money (18 cents) and planned a stop for candy at Priem's store about halfway to the Carp Pond.

This, of course, was in the days before all the concern about the right biking clothes, shoes, or repair kits. We certainly didn't have anything like Camelback hydration systems to prevent us from, God forbid, dehydration. Today, unless we have 1.5 pints of water with us everywhere we go, we will surely turn to dust before the end of the day.

With a hardy breakfast of toasted Wonder Bread and Nestlé chocolate milk put away, I had met Rob on the road. To draw no attention to our scheme, we casually rolled up to the end of the beach. We checked for any neighbors watching, and seeing none, we were off.

Covering that first half-mile past our allowable boundary limit of the beach, we reveled in our newfound freedom and adventure. With as much pride as a couple of 7-year-old boys could puff up in their chests, we had entered uncharted territory, and neither Daniel Boone nor Lewis or Clark could have found anything more thrilling than this, our own journey to see "what was over the next hill."

Peddling past Winnebago Mental Health Institute, several patients working in the large garden yelled to us that our wheels were going backward. They had run toward the road, and we took off in a flurry of fear, as only two young kids who didn't understand mental health issues would do. Spinning our pedals furiously, we were soon at Priem's store. After our perceived escape from attack, we were back in big-boy mode as we marched inside. We placed six red-and-white boxes of Snaps (licorice), 12 Tootsie Roll Midgets, and our 18 cents on the counter, paid in full.

Our last couple of miles toward our destination passed quickly with the consumption of Snaps and Midgets. As we pulled up to the Carp Pond and looked out over Lake Winnebago, it was surely with the same awe and accomplishment that early explorers had felt. A guy working outside had questioned us about where we were from, signaling us to beat a hasty retreat before we were busted, with a call to our parents and God-knows-what punishment: In 1962, our fathers didn't lose any sleep worrying about whether spanking was "politically correct." Tanned hides were still in vogue with parents.

Fueled by candy, we made it back to Winnebago Mental Health Institute, and charged with our memory of the earlier "attack," flew past the hospital at warp speed. We soon neared the beach again, waving to neighbors as we rolled past, both smiling with smugness for the adventure we had just pulled off. Even when Rob's nosy sister Mary Ann had seen the Snaps box in his pocket and wanted to know where he got it, Rob—quick on his feet—stuck the box in his mouth, blew a loud squeal through it, and said he found it on the road. Not a great comeback but definitely annoying enough to make a big sister roll her eyes and leave us alone.

Rob and I went on to share many childhood adventures. Sadly, he died at age 21, but I would always remember that first real bike trip we took. Remembering Rob, I carried a small part of him with me on this big version of the Carp Pond adventure.

WITH THE "Carp Pond Caper" a part of the distant past and me closing in on Oshkosh, my memories fast-forwarded to sharing a meal with a few friends on an evening in late winter of 1979. One of the friends, Steve Katner, had suggested taking a long-distance bike trip that upcoming summer. His thought had been for us to fly to Florida and bike north back to Wisconsin, a trip of about 1,600 miles.

Like most plans hatched over a meal with a couple of beers and in a warm environment with friends, it had been easy to get caught up in the moment. Before I knew it, I was verbally committed to the trip, and we all determined that we would ride the "Minnesota Ironman Bicycle Ride" that April as a training ride in preparation for the Florida trip.

The Ironman is a century (100-mile) ride—a rite of passage into spring and the new bike season for many dyed-in-the-wool bikers. Held in April every year, the ride is attended by thousands of people whose skills range from serious top-level racers, to mom-and-pop types on old Schwinns who have completed the ride for years. The Ironman also attracts a few idiots who get sucked into trying something that they in no way, shape, or form are ready for. Guess where I had fit in at the time?

It had been easy to get caught up in the moment. Before I knew it, I had scraped together the entry fee, and filled out and mailed in the entry form. Only then did my thoughts turn to getting a bike. That's right, getting a bike because I had not ridden a bike a total of 100 miles in the past 10 years combined, much less in one day. My once precious bike had done little but gather dust since I obtained my driver's license.

Having sucked me into this Ironman endeavor, my questionable friends had offered to help me find a good bike. Within two weeks, I became the proud owner of a beautiful, orange Bridgestone Kabuki Diamond Formula. So the time had come, literally, for the rubber to meet the road.

In the month leading up to the Ironman, weather had been unpredictable. It made me think that planning a 100-mile bike ride in Minneapolis, Minnesota, in April made as much sense as planning an outdoor nudist convention at the same time and place. I had probably ridden a grand total of 100 training miles with no ride longer than 20 miles. Should be good to go! And, sure, we had thought it was possible that we would have one of those bluebird, beautiful, sunny spring days; however, in the upper Midwest, we also knew we were more likely to experience something less perfect, if not outright nasty.

ON RACE DAY, Steve, Jerry, and another friend, Al, and I had arrived at the starting line, caught up in the hype of thousands of bikers ready to roll. It had been that hoped-for beautiful blue-sky day, with sunshine yet a brisk 45 degrees at 9:00 A.M. We were sure the temps would warm, and I had worn my cross-country ski outfit topped with a windbreaker, stocking hat, and gloves, and felt ready.

The day was fresh, we were fresh, the adrenaline was pumping, and soon we were 20 miles down the road. With the confidence that only a fool can muster, I congratulated myself on how good this was going. But, in the excitement of the moment, I had ignored what felt like a cool breeze picking up from the north and a few clouds blocking out the sunshine. The day went downhill from there, and trust me, I don't mean rolling easily toward the bottom of a hill. By mile 40, the temperature had continued downward as invading clouds began to drop a cold mist on us, soon developing into a light yet steady rainfall at 40 degrees.

Bikes boxed and gear loaded for trip to airport.

Denise by wall with 4,000 miles to go.

Cascade Mountains, easier to cross by air than by bike.

Eloise and Don Running and our bikes in Washington State—no more gracious hosts anywhere.

Brad, not your ordinary bike tourist, and Denise.

Bob and Dudley, neither of us too thrilled with the other.

Mountain goat at Sperry Chalet in Glacier National Park.

Queen Denise on Lake McDonald in Glacier.

Gary Funk and cattle in Big Sky country, Montana.

Dale and Denise, North Dakota, where the wind blows free.

Dale, Denise, Bob, parting company in Minot, North Dakota.

Welcome to Wisconsin sign. Bob exactly 2,000 miles into the trip.

Like horses hitched at a saloon, our bikes were hitched up at a fruit stand in Ontario.

Pete and Bob with wrench, Rochester, New York. The weight of the wrench was nothing compared to Pete's kindness.

Nathan in tree, Pultneyville, New York. I declined his challenge to race him to the top.

Denise in rain gear. Our gear before today's fancy stuff.

Bob on highway with all four lanes just to ourselves along Lake Ontario.

Boat, 70 feet long and surrounded by 50-year-old trees. Some things are best left a mystery.

Denise with map: "I'm sure this is the best route!"

Maine sign: our last "welcome to" sign.

Denise and lobsters—guess who's coming to dinner!

Denise and Oreos, Maine—our last meal and money on the road.

Bob and Denise, Atlantic Ocean. We started off at the Pacific and ended in the Atlantic.

Car packed: Bob, Denise, and Steve stuffed in like over-packed panniers. Time to head home.

Bob with banjo on bike, Florida to Wisconsin trip, 1980.

Steve, Denise, and Mary Jo (Mathieson), Vera, Dad, and Louis Mathieson, saying good-bye to good friends, Owls Head, Maine.

Nearing the end of the ride through the Hope Landslide mess in British Columbia.

Sperry Chalet work crew, Rose ran a tight ship.

Denise riding into a foggy, smoggy, acid rain day in Ontario.

We stopped briefly at a grocery to buy large trash bags, into which we poked a hole in the bottom for our head and through the sides for our arms—morphing into "Team Hefty."

By mile 60, we could see that many had already dropped from the event, but, of course, in the bravado of youth and pride of stupidity, we forged on. By mile 70, the temperature had dropped into the 30s, and we were no longer able to complain about rain because it had become skin-clinging sleet turning to snow. It had also become apparent to me by mile 50 that, beyond the horrible conditions, every fiber of my body was in a state of rebellion. Consequently, with somewhat open arms, I had welcomed the first stages of hypothermia, which numbed the physical pain in my butt and legs and clouded any mental perception of the agony I was experiencing. By mile 90, I had been reduced to a barely functioning, ice-crusted fool as we forged ahead through a now-steady snowfall. With just a mile to go and a friend on either side of me, each with a hand on my handlebars, we had crossed the finish line.

Getting off my bike, I looked down, surprised to see my seat, as I had been certain it had migrated somewhere about two inches up my butt. I staggered to the truck in the lumbering gait similar to that of Slavomir Rawicz in *The Long Walk* across Siberia. I had little memory of crossing the St. Croix River back into Wisconsin, where my friends deposited me back at my apartment in River Falls. After a 30-minute hot shower, numerous cups of hot chocolate, and a mountain of blankets, I slowly reentered the world of 98.6 degrees.

WITH THAT FREEZING April ride in mind and as I drew closer to my Oshkosh home and Denise, my memories shifted to a third bike trip that paved the way for our cross-continent trek—the Florida trip the previous summer.

Steve and I had approached our Florida trip very differently than Denise and I had prepared for this cross-country trip. For Steve and me, planning had consisted of buying some road maps, throwing a few clothes and a lightweight sleeping bag into our panniers, and counting ourselves good to go. We hadn't bothered with a tent because of the weight, and decided that part of the adventure would be to just ask landowners for permission to roll out our bags. Despite all this concern about weight, I had packed along a five-string banjo. My thought had been that I could pull it out at the end of the day, play a little for people, and maybe pick up a few bucks that would come in handy. I soon realized carrying the weight hadn't been worth the minimal money earned—I was no Earl Scruggs. On top of all that, after biking in 100-degree weather for an average of 115 daily miles, I had been left with little energy at the end of the day for a jam session.

I had decided to ship my banjo back to Wisconsin, and Steve and I continued to crank out big miles in unbelievable heat. Finding it almost impossible to stay hydrated, we had each been drinking two water bottles an hour, in addition to untold cans of cold pop and countless pitchers of water at meal stops. Even with all this, we had never felt as if we were getting enough. At the end of every day, despite often less-than-perfect sleeping conditions, we would fall into a dead-to-the-world coma-like sleep.

WE HAD NOT had any trouble finding places to sleep, as long as we weren't picky—and we certainly were not. Although we had spent one night in a beautiful home in South Carolina, our standard living quarters had revolved more around sleeping under motel canopies, in a church, out in the open, and a couple nights in a jail cell—by choice, not necessity. Well, the first time we stayed in a cell was somewhat by necessity, I guess. Biking through Livingston, Tennessee, a large rainstorm had also moved through. With no tent, we had felt our options were limited. We had stopped at the jail and explained about our trip and predicament. In true southern hospitality fashion, we had been given a cell of our own in which to sleep. Later that evening, as the storm had raged outside, the jailer awakened us and told us he needed our cell for someone who had shot a guy in an argument at the county fair. Intent on taking care of us, he showed us to our new digs for the rest of the night: the drunk tank. It had certainly been no Holiday Inn—just three bare cots and an open toilet. Steve had thrown some aftershave on the walls to kill the smell, but when a large bug crawled across my face an hour later, I grabbed my bags in search of anything else. I had noticed that the jail was attached to the firehouse, and I determined that the neatly folded fire hoses in the back and on top of the fire trucks would make a good campsite for the rest of the evening. From my perch high atop the fire truck nestled comfortably among the fire hoses, I was thankful that no fire calls had come in during the night.

We had pushed hard north leaving behind Florida, Georgia, South Carolina, Tennessee, Kentucky, and finally Indiana as we eventually rode up the west side of Michigan. The days had been a blur of scorching heat and big miles as we rode ourselves into the ground to meet our two-week window of time before Steve had to be back to work. We had arrived late in the day in Ludington, where the Lake Michigan car ferry operates between Wisconsin and Michigan. With the intent of catching the midnight run across the lake, we had celebrated with a large seafood buffet what would be the completion of our trip the following day. We headed for the docks to board the USS *Badger*, with full bellies and a 113-mile day, much of it into headwinds, behind us. The boat pulled out from the docks around 1:00 A.M., and we settled into the passenger lounge area for some rest as we let the boat do the work for these miles.

With the temperature high and the flies thick, I had found it impossible to sleep. I dragged myself out to the open deck, where the brisk breeze in the open air chased away the flies. This certainly hadn't been the Love Boat: This cruise hadn't offered any deck chairs with blankets. So, I had headed back inside, where I came across a pile of large laundry bags that would make a comfy bed, but just as I had settled in, I was informed by a crewmember that regulations wouldn't allow me to block the passageway by sleeping on the bags. I explained how I needed to get some sleep, and he told me cabins were available, which I had to decline, lacking the funds. With a wink and a nod, he opened up one of the doors. Not believing my luck, I had flopped down on the small bunk, muttering my thanks and promising silence as the door closed.

Out of the darkness, I heard, "Maybe you can do something for me."

I bolted upright as the lights came on. Dead tired, confused and momentarily naive, I wondered what I could do for this guy out on Lake Michigan at 2:00 A.M. When he told me what he had in mind my naivety quickly departed. What he had suggested and his manner of doing so was just as inappropriate in 1981 as it would be in 2011. Telling him I was in no way interested, I walked to the door, anxious to exit the situation. When he grabbed my arm to stop me from leaving, it became necessary for me to forcefully deal with him. This guy attempted, through a veiled offer of kindness, to create a scenario favorable to his real intentions. His attempt to prevent me from leaving the room amounted to an assault of which I fortunately got the upper hand. After fumbling with the deadbolt that he had locked, I exited the cabin. I couldn't help but wonder how many times this guy had pulled something like this before with people who were unable to take care of themselves. When on a trip of this nature you come to expect close calls with cars and trucks. This was completely unexpected. In all honesty it irked the hell out of me that the wonderful experience of this trip had to be punctuated with this ugly episode. This guy wasn't just some gay guy attempting to hit on someone. He was a predator, plain and simple.

I found my way back to the passenger area and informed Steve that we would do best to stay awake the rest of this cruise. Within an hour, we docked in Manitowoc, Wisconsin, and with a 70-mile ride that included an unnecessary detour, we found ourselves 1,600 miles from Tallahassee, Florida, our starting point. I was tired, but thrilled at the adventure, which had planted a seed for a cross-continent trip for the summer of 1981.

AS I CLOSED in on Oshkosh and a few days of rest, I tucked away these memories of past expeditions, each of which had played an integral role in this ultimate trip across America. I relied on experiences of each previous journey to shape the next.

As a 7-year-old who would not have been able at that time to explain what had made me want to explore outside of my boundaries, that successful excursion propelled me to stretch those boundaries further. Although one bike trip led to another, each was about so much more than the ride. These trips were about inspiration, tenacity, compromise, and curiosity. The walls of my world were pushed out as I came in contact with a diversity of situations and people that made me stretch myself to a new level. They taught me that life wouldn't always fit into my neat little package and I would at times have to mold myself to fit what I encountered. Other times, I would need to stand my ground in life, or claim my part of the road while on the bike. My journeys on these bicycle trips and those through life can certainly be separated, but I would be a fool to try to convince myself or anyone else that they were not intimately intertwined.

My focus shifted to a couple days of rest, after which Denise and I would embark on the second half of our journey. Despite our experiences to this point, we had no way to predict exactly what lay ahead of us. And therein lay the beauty.

CHAPTER 10

Travelers' Rest

AFTER A DAY of 133 miles, rain, Limburger cheese, and morphing from memories back to real time, I walked through my folks' door and was greeted with the aroma of a home-cooked meal in the oven. The sight of Denise snug on the sofa with a plate of chocolate chip cookies in front of her was definitely encouraging. My brother Jim confirmed my earlier thoughts, saying that Denise had fallen asleep instantly in the car ride from Neillsville to Oshkosh. Since arriving, Denise said her day had revolved around sleep, chocolate chip cookies, sleep, and so on. I knew when I sent her ahead with my brother that my mother Margaret would have her back in good health in short order. Getting me and my two siblings through a myriad of challenges, illnesses, and injuries, my mother could handle anything. Denise already looked healthier, well rested, and pretty well settled in.

I thought it looked like we would be good to go after our two-day planned break. At least that was my hope, although my concern had shifted. After two days of this rest, I wondered if I might need a team of horses to break Denise away from the couch and cookies.

The following day, we reorganized our gear and unpacked some of the things we had shipped back earlier, including the fruit leather. With vivid memories of what a treat it had been when we were wet, tired, and hungry, we tore into the box, anxious to share this discovery with my family. Regaling them with our stories of how delicious it was, we tore off sheets for them to try and enjoy. We waited for confirmation that this was the greatest thing since sliced bread.

"So, hey, how about it, isn't that stuff great?" I asked.

The look on Jim's face was hardly one that said "give me more," and his reply of "It's okay" was not the response I anticipated.

"What do you mean, *okay?*" I asked.

Knowing his taste was dubious at best, I tore off a chunk for myself. Cramming it into my mouth and chewing vigorously, I was ready for the explosion of flavor and energy I remembered from the day we rode out of the rain in the Cascade Mountains after the Hope Slide ride. As I continued chewing and waiting, I glanced around at the others, including Denise, and nobody looked thrilled with this manna from the land of "eh."

I soon realized that like so many things in life, the environment in which something is experienced often affects the perception of its value. Don't get me wrong. Fruit leather was okay, but on the heels of homemade roast chicken with mashed potatoes with gravy, the fruit leather stayed in the box until somewhere down the road when it turned into fruit tin and eventually hit the landfill.

With a couple of days out of the saddle, we spent an inordinate amount of time resting and eating. By this point in the trip, my weight was down to about 170 pounds, truly my fighting weight. A picture taken of me at that low body weight is the only proof that I actually had visible abs in my life.

With the extra time, I had the bright idea that a good activity during our rest days would be to do a little waterskiing. When only Denise and I were around the house, we lowered the boat into the water. As I drove, Denise was first up.

Lake Winnebago tends to have strong algae blooms in the summer; once we were about a mile offshore, I realized this day's thick pea-green water was no exception. I could see disgust on Denise's face as I pulled her through it. I knew that as long as she didn't fall, she would be okay, and I turned the boat for home—until a boat pulled alongside us with a flashing light and a guy in a uniform. Busted! I knew we were supposed to have a spotter in the boat, but I had figured we could get away with a few spins around the bay. Wrong! I knew a fine was coming my way, although it would be nothing compared to Denise's punishment as she slowly descended into the disgusting green soup.

Denise swam to the boat, and as I helped her in, I knew it would be best not to comment about how the slime was not only colorful, but also smelled of rotting seaweed. As Denise began scraping the green goo from her body, I explained to the Department of Natural Resources warden about our bike trip and this break, hoping that he would be enthralled with our story and cut us a break in the process. It turned out he was really amazed to hear about our ride. After a number of questions and exclamations from him, I knew I had saved us from a fine. He wished us well, started to shove off, and handed me a ticket for $31.00 for having no spotter in the boat. With a wave, he was on his way.

Turning to show Denise the ticket, hoping for some sympathy, the green shimmer on her skin and hair and the odor of the rotting seaweed emanating from her reminded me that I had better watch my step or incur further penalty.

AS WE CONTEMPLATED starting again, my brother Jim gave some serious consideration to joining us for the last part of the trip. We both would have loved to have him along, and he came very close, but decided against it in the end. Now it was back to me, Denise, and Steve, who would be joining us the following morning for our departure.

When I had wheeled into Oshkosh a couple days earlier, I had wondered if starting out again would be difficult following such a nice break. After a month of hard riding, one becomes fairly worn out and looks forward to the chance to rest and rebuild. Surprisingly, our recovery was fast after a couple of days of long rests and good, home-cooked meals. We were actually restless to hit the road again. At this point, our trip had become a lifestyle and as such, riding was the norm, and the days off, the exception.

CHAPTER 11

Shifting Gears

COMING OFF A three-day break, Denise was back to 100 percent and I felt great. With a quick good-bye to my folks, we got a 5:30 A.M. start for the 70-mile ride to Manitowoc, Wisconsin, where we would board the ferry. We didn't need to be there until noon, but we didn't want to get caught in any headwinds or detours because we'd have a 24-hour wait for the next boat if we missed this one. We had thought about heading north and riding around Lake Michigan via Canada, but we wanted to bike through a good portion of Michigan and not just the Upper Peninsula. This would also be more direct by several hundred miles, and I needed to make sure I was back at my school bus driving job before the end of August. Each added day also meant added expenses.

To get to Manitowoc, we first needed to travel around Lake Winnebago, which is over 30 miles long and 10 miles wide. Jim and my close friend Shawn James joined us for the day as we headed down the road through Neenah and Menasha to once again hit Highway 10.

Shawn and I had shared many mini-adventures over the years, mostly centered around cross-country skiing or white-water kayaking. In 1978, Shawn and I decided to ski the American Birkebeiner, a 55-kilometer, extremely challenging ski race, just two weeks after our first cross-country skiing attempt. We had headed for Mount Telemark in northwestern Wisconsin after borrowing my father's pickup truck with a shell topper on the back. We had picked up our bibs, and then had retired to the back of the pickup to try to sleep.

It had been the end of February and the nighttime temperatures had dropped down to 5 degrees above zero, chilly to say the least. During the evening, the race staff had attempted to empty the parking lot, but we had kept quiet when they knocked on our truck. To our good fortune, they had left us alone, and we awoke in the morning with a parking spot only 100 yards from the site of the mass start.

Both of us finished, and despite having been dog-tired, we had danced and partied the night away at the Telemark Lodge. I was happy Shawn was joining us for this short ride over to Lake Michigan. Sharing segments of such an important trip with good friends and my brother enhanced the experience so much.

AS WE LEFT the Neenah-Menasha area, we had a very close call that could well have ended the trip. Although the road had a broad paved shoulder, we chose to stretch out single file because of the traffic, and I brought up the end of the line. A large truck carrying a load of scrap construction supplies passed me and then Denise. I watched helplessly as his load shifted and a long two-by-eight board slid partially off the truck and stuck out about six feet from the right side as the truck approached Jim. Neither Jim nor the driver had any idea of what had occurred. Denise and I both yelled as loud as we could, and Jim looked back just in time to duck down and miss the board's blow to the head by mere inches. I knew that this was truly a brush with death, as the truck had been traveling over 30 MPH. Fortunately, the truck driver also caught sight of the board in his mirror before he passed Shawn and Steve.

As with any close call, we assessed the situation to see if we could have done anything differently, which in this case, we couldn't have, and then shook it off and kept going. The concerns some expressed prior to the start of our trip were valid. Thousands of cars would pass within inches as we traveled coast to coast, and unforeseen incidents like that would happen. We each needed to decide for ourselves if the reward potential of such a journey outweighed the inherent risks.

In this case, we were wise to have chosen single-file riding and to have kept an eye on one another to dodge a bullet. Jim, who came close to losing his head, summed it up best in his usual unexcited demeanor. "Close only counts in horseshoes!"

WE ARRIVED AT the dock with plenty of time to spare, and purchased our tickets right away. It was evident that this midday trip was going to be much more crowded than the midnight trip of the previous year before. At $16.45 each, the tickets took a good chunk of our money, but it was probably the best deal of the trip relative to the mileage it saved us from biking around the lake into Canada.

Prior to checking our bikes in with the cargo handlers, I rummaged into my front handlebar pack for my camera and some maps that I wanted to review during the crossing. I pulled my hand out wet, but didn't give it a lot of thought as I zipped my pack shut. Because it was another very hot day, sweat was running down my forehead into my eyes, and as I reached up to wipe it from my eyes, I realized too late my mistake. Not since I had survived the "night of the grizzly attack" in Glacier National Park had I even thought about the small spray can of mace in my pack. As I became reduced to a fountain of flowing, burning tears in seconds, I realized I had accidentally sprayed the mace onto my fingers and then wiped it directly into my eyes, assuring myself of at least 20 minutes of misery.

I could tell from the expressions of one nearby couple that they thought that I really was sad to leave my friends as we boarded the ship. While my tears and sinus mucus really let go, we all said our good-byes, and the ferry pulled away from the dock. We watched Jim and Shawn as they rode onto the breakwater, waved, and sent us on our way as we began the next segment of our trip. It was a bright, warm day as we cleared the harbor. The wind was slight with a tailwind, and small waves assisted us across Lake Michigan. With over a hundred people on board, in daylight and fair weather, it was a far cry from the miserable crossing of the previous year.

We arrived at Ludington dock at 5:30 P.M., having lost an hour when we switched time zones, claimed our bikes and gear, and took off. Leaving the dock, I spotted a fish house, and couldn't resist the opportunity to grab some smoked fish and crackers for dinner. Smoked fish was a favorite of mine, but not particularly of Denise's or Steve's, so I feigned an apologetic front while inwardly rejoicing, thinking "all the more for me."

On a map of Michigan, Ludington sat about two-thirds of the way north up the west side of the state. Few sizeable towns were nearby, the only choices being north or south on Highway 31 to either Traverse City or Muskegon, respectively. We chose to jump on our familiar friend Highway 10 heading east, and start across Michigan on our way to the U.S.-Canadian border at the cities of Port Huron, Michigan, and Sarnia, Ontario.

With a pretty good road and little traffic, Denise and I were back into the flow of our trip. It became evident, however, that Steve was not up for being on this highway and suggested we find some back roads. Just the suggestion of "back roads" set me back a bit. I recalled family car trips in the 1960s, on which my father liked to try the "back roads." One time, we ended up on a road called Phantom Canyon that terrified me so much that I transferred the image of the Royal Gorge Bridge from my jackknife onto my sweaty palm. A back road experiment that goes wrong in a car is easily corrected in effortless minutes, whereas it could consume hours of time and a lot of energy on bicycle. Although I do advocate about how the soul of a trip lies in the journey, I'm also a fan of direct routes and an opponent of backtracking.

Making a brief stop in the town of Scottville, we hit the bakery where I pounded down my umpteenth Long John. Although I realized they provided minimal nutritional value, they certainly earned their place on the comfort food list. Bakery stops had seemed to become the standard operating procedure, and we were drawn to them like moths to bike lights. At the time, I thought about planning another ride that could be called *Long Johns across America,* and I could rate them on a scale of 1 to 10. I would have rated the Scottville Long John an 8 out of 10.

Following Steve's lead, we turned off Highway 10, searching for a better route. Looking at a map of Michigan in 1981, you would have seen that the area we headed into was mostly wild countryside. I had to concede that the traffic was light, in fact virtually nonexistent, probably because nobody lived there. And no one lived there probably because these roads received little or no maintenance, or at least that's what my kidneys led me to believe as they rattled around like dice. We had not traveled more than a few miles north when we turned onto another questionable road heading east. As the already-rough pavement gave way to gravel, my gut feelings also began to surface. By this point, Denise and I had biked well over 2,000 miles, and we had become pretty good at listening to our instincts. Although Steve still wanted to forge ahead, I had my doubts, especially because our maps did not even show the road we were on. When an old, beat-up car came by, I took the opportunity to flag down the driver and ask some questions. After a brief introduction, I asked Matthew, the driver, "Where will this road take us?"

Responding to a question with a question, with which I was not thrilled, he replied, "Where do you want to go?"

Fighting the urge to snap back with an agitated, "Where do you think I want to go?" I reminded myself that I was a visitor in need, and instead responded, "Eventually to Port Huron."

The look on Matthew's face told me all I needed to know, "You can't get there from here. Why didn't you take Highway 10?"

Giving me the answer I knew in my heart and expected, and managing to deliver it as a question just made my day.

In that instant, I knew Denise and I needed to stay true to ourselves and our way of traveling. We had come too far to adapt a different strategy, and if we did, I knew it would set a sour tone for both of us. I didn't want to appear selfish, but this was the trip we had planned, and we needed to be comfortable with the manner in which we proceeded. After a brief discussion, we all agreed backtracking would be best. Within about an hour, we found ourselves back at our cutoff point on Highway 10.

I would be a liar if I didn't admit to being pissed off that we had just spent two hours going nowhere. I knew from talking with Denise that she felt the same as I did, but neither of us wanted this to blow up into a big issue. I knew Steve had realized that I wasn't happy with the situation, and I'm sure he himself had doubts as to whether he wanted to travel in the manner to which we had become accustomed.

Back on our eastward track, we bumped into a couple of other bikers, Gary and Sharon, who started their trip in Oregon and were heading for New York. Gary lived in Honolulu, Hawaii, where he was a teacher. He expressed how much he was enjoying being "off the island." It made me think that no matter how nice a place may be, even a paradise surrounded by water could feel like a prison.

Biking together 25 miles to just outside of Farwell, Michigan, we came upon a tremendous roadside fruit stand that two sisters ran for their parents. We loaded up on fresh produce, and the girls invited us to set up our tents inside their father's new pole shed, which still had fresh grass under it. With new friends, fresh food, 86 more miles behind us, and a safe haven to spend the night, I felt the troubles of the day fade. While night closed in, I hoped that we would be able to find a doable route that wouldn't result in hard feelings for anyone.

THE FOLLOWING MORNING, we were at it by 6:20 A.M. After having enjoyed a few days off plus the day that included a ferry ride, I half expected we would need a little time to get back in the groove again. I had come to realize that my issues with Steve's route choice the previous day had as much to do with me as they did him. Thinking about it the previous night, I concluded that if Steve and I had started this trip together as we had the previous year, we would have found common ground in approaching the situation. I believed no one was at fault in the issue, but that Denise and I had already established an approach. This wasn't to say we couldn't and wouldn't compromise, but we had a game plan that had worked well for us thus far, and we both agreed we wanted to stick with it.

Gary and Sharon decided to ride with us again, and we all stopped for breakfast in Farwell. This proved to be the start of a not-too-easy day. With five of us, the stop dragged out way too long; by the time we were finished, it was 9:30, and we had only put in a few miles for the day. I felt myself getting edgy, and it seemed to set the tone for the day.

Leaving town, I noticed that the surrounding area looked and felt to be going through rough economic times. Although this part of our ride was quite rural and sparsely populated, we were headed toward the much larger city of Flint, Michigan. We spoke with a few local folks who confirmed that the area had few jobs for young people in the area. The car industry, once Michigan's bright star, had already started to falter at the time, and many of the once almost-guaranteed jobs in the auto industry had disappeared.

It was evident that road maintenance was one area lacking the attention it needed. The road heading south to Frankenmuth was riddled with cracks and potholes. And it wasn't just the road surface that got worse; I could feel my attitude deteriorating as well. It started with my discovery that the bumpy road had claimed two of my best souvenirs of the trip, one being my "Stampede" T-shirt given to me at the rodeo in Wolf Point, Montana, and the other the flag I had carried on my bike since Glacier National Park. I had stuffed the shirt in my helmet that I had attached to the seat post. The flag was propped in one of the ventilation holes in the same helmet. Obviously, the constant shaking on the bumpy road had jarred both loose. Somewhere in this loss, I'm sure there's a lesson about always wearing your helmet!

Monetarily, neither was a big deal, but I felt a real sense of loss as I had brought these two items so far, not to mention that I believed the flag caused many passing drivers to give us our space. I decided to backtrack about two miles, hoping to find them, but I had no such luck. I started to feel guilty that I had held up the show, so I returned to the group. We all proceeded down the bumpy roadway, and it wasn't long before I heard that distinct and all-too-familiar sound of a breaking spoke. Fortunately, I could pull a wheel, replace a spoke, pump up the tire, and true the wheel in record time by this point. This was no big deal for someone who had practiced it as much as I had in the past month, and we were soon back in the saddle, headed down Highway 83. Twenty-two miles after the broken spoke, I heard another memorable sound: the *pffft* of a deflating tire. Once again, I changed the tire in no time flat (pun intended). On days like this, on such a trip, I told myself that the trick was not to let it get me down too much, a trick I hadn't quite mastered yet.

Well into the afternoon and having traveled 77 miles, we decided to call it a day at the town of Frankenmuth, Michigan. Despite a group of five with three tents and no campground nearby, we eventually found a nice park with a lot of trees, where we rolled our bikes down into a secluded area and set up our tents. We hadn't seen any signs indicating a camping area, but we also hadn't seen any "No Camping" signs, so we rationalized that we would be okay and hoped for the best.

From the looks of things in town, Frankenmuth residents were obviously proud of their German heritage, and they had woven into it a commercialization of Christmas in July. A very tidy town, Frankenmuth had created a tourist mecca, attracting people to visit and shop with Santas in lederhosen.

Tired yet happy that a tough day was behind us, we decided to enjoy a little night on the town. Being more than a little concerned about our camp and gear, we relocated everything to a grove of dense pine trees that hid our tents. Hoping for the best, we rode into town and found an authentic-looking German bar.

Despite sharing a German heritage, all five of us were happy to see that the bar also served Italian—a waiter with a practiced hand drifted by with a large pizza and a tray full of beer steins. The place was loud, packed with patrons, and filled with aromas of good food. We felt right at home. Within a short time, the beer and pizza erased the day's edge. After satisfying our hydration and carbohydrate needs, we took the chance to talk about and resolve a few differences, and devise a game plan for the rest of the trip.

It had become obvious that we all had different views on how to travel relative to route, mileage, and road selection.

We agreed that there really was no right or wrong way, and that it was important that we all needed to feel comfortable with our choices, as much as possible.

Despite our differences, we were enjoying one another's company. Gary and Sharon were very nice people. Like us, they had been on the road for a long time. Steve was also a great guy, and was just beginning his trip, which would be about two weeks in all. Steve's preferences were more aligned with those of Gary and Sharon. Because of this, Steve decided to tag along with them for a number of days.

We arranged to meet up at a few tentative checkpoints along the way, playing it by ear and recognizing the potential for misses in the scheduled meet-ups. We all felt comfortable with the choice. If all else failed, we planned to meet at a friend's home in Owls Head, Maine, on approximately August 10. Our first meeting place was to be at the customs checkpoint where we would cross into Canada. Although we were following different routes, the customs check seemed a surefire rendezvous point, as it was only about a 70-mile ride from Frankenmuth, and was the only entrance into Canada.

We were back at our campsite at 10:30 P.M., relieved to find everything safe and secure. As Denise and I mentally prepared to leave Michigan and enter Canada again, we found it almost hard to believe that we began this trip in Canada 2,600 miles ago. Those early days and the first diffi-cult miles in nonstop rain and cool weather in British Columbia seemed a distant memory. The following day, we would ride into Canada through Sarnia, Ontario, where we planned to spend an evening with Steve's aunt, uncle, and their family. There we would firm up the tentative plans we had made at the bar.

AFTER OUR NIGHT out in Frankenmuth, we were all ready to hit the bikes surprisingly early, and by 7:30 A.M., we had left camp and rolled up to a diner for a quick breakfast special. After washing down a great breakfast of several Long Johns and juice, we were good to go.

At this stage of our trip, we consumed food in almost unbelievable quantities. There was just no way that we were able to keep pace with the caloric demands of long mileage, day in and out. For Denise and me, our food limits were set only by our budgets, and I can't imagine how much we would have eaten in a day if our funds had been unlimited. It was probably good that neither of us had a credit card, because if we had, we would probably have found ourselves in debtor's prison at the trip's conclusion, and it would all have been for food. I had to admit to being envious of Steve who had already graduated, was employed, and traveled with the benefit of a credit card. Not only did it eliminate his need to carry as much cash, but it also allowed him to treat himself along the way and provided a safety net if problems had come up.

One morning, as we contemplated our dwindling money, Denise asked, "What do you think it would be like on the trip if we had unlimited funds?"

Giving thought to Denise's question, I responded, "I think we'd take advantage of a lot more motel nights rather than camping, and I know I'd be eating a lot more food. I'm glad we don't have the option."

"I wouldn't want to do that right now either," she replied. I'd met few people in life who could have held a candle to Denise's tenacity. She was as far from being a "fluff" chick as she could possibly be.

"Don't get me wrong," she continued. "Down the road when we're old, in our 50s or 60s, I would hope we are still doing things like this. But then it would be nice to be able to take it easier and maybe even be able to make side trips along the way and afford to visit more local places that we can't right now."

With a total of less than $500.00 between the two of us at the start of our trip, we continually gave strong consideration to each expenditure. Although I could have borrowed some extra cash from my family, I would not have been comfortable with that. Having met many folks also biking along the way, we had a firsthand opportunity to see a broad variety of ways people chose to approach their travel. Some were just like us, confined to a tight budget, whereas others, like Bert who we met in Glacier, were older, well established, and could afford motels and meals at restaurants every day. We all shared the same love for biking and, as such, had that common denominator. But in my mind, I knew that a trip like ours was different from a well-financed trip. We didn't have any backups if things didn't go right. Our approach may have caused us to proceed with a more conservative approach than would have been the case if we had been flush with cash.

Doing the trip in the manner in which we did, at that time of our lives, is not something I would trade for anything. I have always appreciated the things in my life that came with hard work and some struggle. Having limited options was an advantage. Our trip required us to be more creative, adventurous, and dependent on each other. Even though our 50s and 60s were then 30-plus years away, this experience would set the tone for our lives later. Although I enjoyed the thought of a trip full of warm motel rooms with showers, and restaurants with hot, good food served to us, I hoped that even when we enjoyed those comforts in future trips, we would treasure the memories of that summer in 1981. They were built around our Eureka tent, cozy sleeping bags, soup and sandwiches warmed by a small cook stove, and two bicycles.

BEFORE LEAVING FRANKENMUTH and heading for Ontario, we couldn't resist making one stop at a Christmas shop, just for a quick look. Those folks seemed to have the commercialization part of Christmas nailed; from moving reindeer and blow-up Santas, to a gazillion aromatic candles ready to infuse one's home with any and every holiday scent imaginable. Moving through the aisles with a large contingent of grandmotherly types, most wearing shirts with cute little critters appliquéd on them, I actually enjoyed myself in a weird way. A self-admitted holiday junkie, I was reminded of many past Christmas shopping trips with my family as a youngster in Wisconsin. A Scotch pine–scented candle had me convinced for a moment that the artificial tree in front of me was real. A young woman dressed as an elf snapped me back to the fact that it was July, and not December. She didn't look like any of the elf depictions I remembered seeing, and I doubt Santa would have ever left his shop if all his workers looked like her.

Leaving behind Christmas in July, we headed our bikes south on Highway 83 until we hit Highway 54 and then Highway 57, which carried us through to Columbiaville. This is where Steve, Gary, and Sharon chose to take a different route because they felt the highway was a bit too busy, even though their chosen course added extra miles.

The route we selected was really pretty nice. We took a country road that paralleled Highway 21 for 14 miles and then cut back up to 21. There, we found a three-foot shoulder, smooth and paved outside of the white line. In addition to a good road with light traffic, we also once again caught a tailwind. Riding tailwinds versus pushing against headwinds was the equivalent to coasting downhill versus climbing uphill, or paddling downriver versus upriver.

Like any of these more challenging alternatives, riding into headwinds is no big deal when done in small doses, but confronting those face-first gusts for eight to ten hours a day, on several consecutive days, they significantly cut deep into the core of one's muscles and even deeper into one's attitude. Focusing on anything but the relentless grind becomes difficult. A 25-mile ride into the wind can leave one spent; a 50-mile ride on tailwinds can leave one looking for more.

All too often on long bike rides, no matter what circuit of turns or curves I took, I seemed to find myself perpetually headed into the wind. Those were the days that I used all those gears that nonriders had pointed at and asked, "Who needs all those? I'm good with my one speed." Those folks need to ride Highway 2 in North Dakota, heading west into that howling beast. Crossing the country on a one-speed bike would be like going through life with only one answer for every obstacle in front of you. You might get by, but the journey would probably involve some pain, and you might find yourself blown backward.

CHAPTER 12

Oh, Canada

THE BLUE WATER BRIDGE serving as the gateway between Port Huron, Michigan, and Sarnia, Ontario, loomed
before us as we prepared to enter Canada once again.
Rolling over its 6,000 feet of length and peering down from
200 feet above water level, we knew it was easily the largest
bridge crossing since day one of our trip, when we illegally
crossed the bridge from Vancouver Island to mainland British
Columbia. Unlike that day of rain, cold, and trepidation,
though, this day we basked in sunshine and blue skies as we
crossed over the St. Clair River. And although hundreds of
cars again whizzed by within inches of us, we were no longer
the somewhat timid riders of day one but were now seasoned
veterans with over 3,000 miles tucked in our panniers.

We had agreed to meet Steve at the Canadian border,
which was only about a 55-mile ride. We cruised, with good
road conditions and a nice breeze, but as did every state,
Michigan threw us a curve with another broken spoke just
ten miles from the border. Despite this, we still pulled into

customs at 7:00 P.M., and with a limited check, we were waved through into Canada.

After a brief 15-minute wait, we saw Steve pull up. However, his luck was still somewhere down the road behind him. Whether just luck of the draw or whether the customs agent saw something he didn't like, Steve received the royal treatment. Whereas Denise and I had just been asked to answer a few questions, Steve had to unpack his panniers and pack, pull the end plugs from his handlebars, and pull his seat post out for inspection. He had nothing to worry about; even so, the guards had a way of making even innocent people felt guilty with their steely-eyed stares, terse responses, and doubtful looks.

Once Steve was cleared and had repacked his gear, we took off to find his relatives, Jerry and Lea Grevstad of Sarnia, Ontario.

Although we arrived at the Grevstads' home relatively late in the day, that did not stop them from welcoming us with open arms and an unbelievable feast of steak, corn on the cob, and ice cream. One of Steve's young cousins was amazed at the amount of food we ate. We'd come to realize that we had to consciously focus on being polite and attentive to people who invited us to meals. Refueling became such a primary role, and when we were treated to special meals that went far beyond our typical daily fare, we easily forgot the fact that it was rude to only show people the top of our heads at meals.

The food was tremendous, and learning about the lives of a Canadian family was interesting. With Canadians being our close, friendly neighbors, we seem to take one another for granted. Although we share so many similarities, we also have different lifestyles, mannerisms, and government formats. Our late arrival, large meal, and hot shower cut our visit short. We were all ready to call it a night.

AT 7:00 A.M. the next morning, I awoke from one of those deep sleeps in which I realized I had never moved all night. After our good-byes and thanks, we were back on the road by 8:30. We met up with Gary and Sharon, and after a brief discussion and a look at the maps, we again decided to take separate routes. They had plans to visit friends, and their route was about 110 miles, much more than Denise and I planned to ride that day, particularly when part of their route led us out of our way.

We made our arrangements, and agreed to get in touch with Steve to establish a possible connection. In those days before cell phones we took our chances when trying to connect at a particular place and time.

We headed out on the Queens Highway 7, picked up Highway 81 swinging south of London, and then jumped on Highway 3. This route traveled almost directly east and was lightly traveled: Most of the communities along the way were small and rural. We traveled roughly parallel to the north shore of Lake Erie, generally about 20 miles from the lakeshore.

Taking a brief rest along the way, we were approached by some workers from a tobacco farm. One of them, Paul, was particularly interested in our trip. Giving him details of our travels, we could see in his eyes that he wished he could bike with us. He explained that he had competed as a bike racer for years in his youth. He had also done some trips, none approaching the length of ours, but he had always wanted to do a longer trip. Paul was in his 40s and had a family. He said he had no time or money to even think about a trip. As we talked and shared, it was easy to imagine Paul in his earlier days. By his questions and intense interest, we felt him almost become a part of the ride. Passing his hands over our bikes and commenting about our gearing, wheels, and so on, a biker emerged whose soul had been covered by the responsibilities of life.

Before we parted, Paul talked of pulling out the old bike that he hadn't ridden in years. He thought it was time to get his family involved in riding. To see the way his face glowed as he described his past biking days and how he contemplated starting anew left me feeling that we may have rekindled a spark. Funny how a person can roll into a complete stranger's life and, in the span of just a few minutes, make a connection that is much more than just passing. I probably would never know, but in my heart, I hoped Paul found a way to get back on the road and still chase his dreams as we were able to.

Continuing east on Highway 3, we were met with a beautiful day of sunshine. For most of our trip, we had exceptional weather, with only a few early days of rain and cold. Far and away, the tailwinds had outpaced the headwinds. Such days made me wish the trip would never end.

We had become so well adjusted to this lifestyle that we often anticipated what each was feeling. In the early days on the trail, we had fallen into a pattern of who would do what, as far as tasks were concerned. In the beginning, setting up the tent was a somewhat awkward exercise, but it had evolved into a two-minute process of me unrolling the tent and Denise assembling the poles—and we were finished. As one of us fired up the stove, the other prepared whatever simple food we were having. We became very efficient, and if it weren't for the lack of funds, we would probably have kept right on moving up the coast of Maine all the way to Newfoundland. This gypsy lifestyle saturated our blood, and I wondered from time to time how difficult it would be to finish abruptly and jump right back into the life of a student with a tightly scheduled day, papers to write, tests to study for, and a job driving school bus.

Just outside of Shedden, Ontario, we met another couple on a bike trip from Oregon to New York. Jon and Melissa Beamer were teachers and, like ourselves, were nearing the end of their trip. Having just gotten back into biking our own pace and style, it was with a little trepidation that we decided to join them when they invited us to do so. In no time at all, however, we found ourselves really enjoying their company. As we biked through the beautiful Ontario countryside, we enjoyed sharing trip stories. When we mentioned the cattle stampede and rodeo ride in Montana, Denise and I were officially dubbed "Dale and Roy" of Evans and Rogers fame. We were about the same ages, and found ourselves swapping childhood memories that included raucous renditions of "Happy Trails to You," "Rawhide," and "Bum da da, Bum da da, Bum da da Bum Bonanza." Melissa and Denise broke into a hilarious rendition of, "I said to myself, vas is das here, das is my top-notcher, my mama dear…Top-notcher, horn blower, inky dinky do, dats vat ve learned in dat school yahoo." Writing this, I realize that it might have been one of those times when you needed to be there, but for the four of us, thousands of miles from home, we sang with gusto, oblivious to the possibility that someone might hear us.

Along the way, we passed by some old abandoned homes. It was obvious no one had lived in them for quite some time, as the weeds were knee-high, doors and windows hung open, and fresh paint hadn't been seen in decades. The architecture of these homes was beautiful, with elaborate woodwork accentuating the structures. We wondered what dreams had first brought people to this rural area to build homes only to later be abandoned. It reminded us of the cabin remnants in Washington and Idaho that had once been someone's dreams, but that had been left empty when realities of life overshadowed earlier hopes.

Later in the day, we came across a baseball park with bathrooms and running water. After some local folks had told us that we were welcome to make camp there, we set about preparing for a shared meal of pasta, salad, and French bread. With the benefit of two stoves blazing, four sets of hands preparing, and a bottle of wine and a six pack of beer, we settled in for a grand meal fit for royalty. It included an encore performance of the songs from earlier in the day. Sharing our meal, stories, and songs with our new friends, I realized that riding as a group is great as long as the individuals are on a similar page. With full bellies, great company, and a few liquid refreshments, we all agreed that it was a day to remember. As our small fire died down, the day's ride caught up with us, as did the mosquitoes. We bid our friends goodnight and settled in.

AFTER THE PREVIOUS night's feast, the following morning's breakfast of leftover cold spaghetti definitely fell a few notches lower on the likeability scale. With a brisk morning but a rising sun promising another great day, we were all on the road by 8:30, and the miles passed quickly. We jogged around the town of Shedden to Highway 16 and then jumped off onto Highway 45 to Highway 1, which brought us into Simcoe, the town where we were planning to meet Steve and company. As we stopped for a brief rest along the way, a farmer with a truckload of fresh-picked cucumbers stopped to chat. When he prepared to take off, he gave us a pack full of cucumbers. What seemed an odd offering turned out to be quite a treat. As the day warmed, the cucumbers were refreshing snacks to munch on; until then, I had never given any thought to the phrase "cool as a cucumber." But cool they were, and although perhaps not nutritionally balanced like high-energy snack bars, the lowly, simple cucumbers were just the ticket.

When we arrived in Simcoe, it was obvious a community celebration was in progress. With all the businesses closed, people were in the street enjoying a parade, food booths, and various contests. Wandering through the maze of activities, we bumped into a large group of cyclists from Oregon who were on a commercial group trip. While Jon and Melissa chatted with their state mates, we headed off to the food tents—the biggest part of any celebration, be it in the United States, Canada, or just about any country.

It struck me that food was probably the greatest single diplomatic tool of the world. We share meals in our homes, we break bread in churches, our industries offer company picnics, and our governments have state dinners. Throughout our trip, meals had often been our introduction to the people we'd met. Although I'm certain that any number of nutritionists would have told me that two bratwursts with kraut and a cold beer were not the optimum meal fare following a long day of biking, I put practicality aside and followed my gut (pun intended). Just as my stinky Limburger cheese lunch in Fremont, Wisconsin, paved the way to a visit with old-timers in a bar on a rainy day, the day's brats and beer were perfect icebreakers to spending a few hours with our Canadian neighbors.

We touched base with Steve again, and learned that he had decided to continue on with Gary and Sharon for a while longer. We decided to just meet up at the end in Owls Head, Maine. Although this was not at all the way we thought things would work out, this was just another adjustment and seemed to be an arrangement that suited each of us.

Meeting back up with Jon and Melissa, it was obvious they were having a great time.

"You guys won't believe what happened to us," Melissa said. "We were eating with some townspeople who asked about our trip."

Jon added, "When hearing we were passing through on our way from Oregon to New York, they kidnapped us."

"It turns out that every year during this celebration, they 'kidnap' some visitors who then become the guests of the town," Melissa finished.

With celebrity status, our friends were now the recipients of lodging, meals, and a host of other treats. Having been selected as royalty, they only had a short time before they had to leave for their first obligation as town guests. We all felt some regret that our time together was ending rather abruptly. They felt somewhat guilty that their celebrity status didn't include us, and we had to admit feeling a bit jealous. However, we were happy for our friends. In many ways, this experience was similar to our rodeo adventure in Wolf Point, Montana. That had been a great time for us and truly an experience we would remember for a lifetime. This was an opportunity for our friends to have the same, and we were happy for them. Once again we had biked into, and now out of, the lives of two kindred souls. In only a couple of days, we shared experiences that would stay with us forever, even if we never met again. We wished them well and safe travels, and headed east, knowing that our trip was rapidly winding down. We would cross back into the states in another day.

With a bit of a late start out of town and bellies full of bratwursts, we weren't breaking any speed records. The sky was a bit hazy with a slight mist in the air, just enough to make things damp. The sun was trying to break through the haze and, I was hoping, end this misty condition. As we biked along, I kept trying to wipe away the rain that ran into my eyes and caused them to sting. Although not terrible, it was certainly annoying and uncomfortable, causing me to blink constantly. A short distance down the road, we stopped for a short break at a filling station, and as I talked with the man running things, we inevitably discussed the weather.

"I'm hoping that sun breaks through these clouds and dries things up," I commented.

"This is how it is most days around here," the guy offered. "Those clouds are pollution from Toronto just north of here."

I looked at the sky, and realized my mistake in thinking the clouds blocking the sun were clouds of nature. In reality, they were a combination of pollutants from industrial plants burning fossil fuels. The stinging that had bothered my eyes all morning had actually been caused by acid rain, the mist that we had been riding through.

I had been reading about acid rain for years, but this was the first time I had actually been amid it. Even though the problem was real, only a small part of the population realized it and many others tended to be apathetic. Just because I didn't live where an oil spill washed ashore didn't mean it wouldn't affect me or that I had no responsibility.

A short ride of another 20 more miles brought us close to 100 miles for the day. At Jarvis, Ontario, we stopped after

Earl and Jean Makey invited us to spend the night at their home. Earl and Jean seemed to be in about their late 60s or early 70s, and welcomed the chance for company. Their old farmhouse had been their home for decades, and our visit made obvious that time and change had left the Makeys feeling pushed aside and left behind. They shared with us stories of earlier days when times were better, things moved slower, and friends and relatives were closer. They felt alone and isolated, yet they had nowhere to go or money to do so. As they presented a simple meal to us, I really appreciated their willingness to share what they did have. They showed us our room for the evening, where we found a soft, comfortable bed. While preparing to turn in, we heard a knock at our door. I opened the door and found Jean Makey waiting.

"I almost forgot to give you this. With the rain and all, it's not a great night for a trip outside."

Jean handed me an odd porcelain bowl and bid us goodnight.

I approached Denise. "I guess this is for us to wash up or something."

I had not realized what I had in my hands until Denise pointed out, "I don't think you'll want to put your face in that! It's a chamber pot."

"A what?"

"It's a chamber pot that you use if you need a bathroom trip during the night."

Quickly setting down this portable toilet, I rubbed my hands on my pants and just looked at Denise.

"What?"

"They don't have indoor toilets. They have an outhouse, and that's what she meant about not a great night for a trip outside."

The situation came into focus for me, and I knew with my whole heart that there was no way on God's green earth that I was going to use that pot. The pot looked far more decorative than need be considering its intended use, and it was with dread that I felt the first rumbling from my stomach. Just like you never have to sneeze until you're someplace where you don't want to sneeze, I now found myself recounting my somewhat gluttonous day with the bratwurst and kraut. With fear supported by intestinal rumbling, I anticipated the worst.

"I don't care if it turns into a tornado outside, it's the outhouse for me before that thing," particularly as I glanced around the room. I realized that if I were to need it, God forbid, where would I do so? I couldn't even picture the whole scenario, and quite honestly didn't want to. As Denise gave me one of her best "whatever" looks and seemingly fell right to sleep, I gingerly picked up the "pot" and placed it into the farthest corner of the room. While I laid in bed, I couldn't help but ponder possibilities.

I finally closed my eyes to sleep, with a parting thought that I would not want it to be my night to wash dishes if chamber pots were included.

WITH A SURPRISINGLY terrific, and yes uninterrupted, sleep, I felt great the next morning as I jogged down the stairs, out the door, and into the outhouse. I had never thought I would appreciate an outhouse as I did when I considered the chamber pot option. The Makeys served us a quick breakfast, and we parted ways, promising to send a postcard when we reached Maine. I was touched by the generosity of strangers who, despite having little, were so willing to open their doors and share what they did have with us, chamber pot notwithstanding.

With a 6:00 A.M. wake-up, we were on the road before 7. We had plenty of time to enjoy a leisurely pace through the last stretch of Ontario, and hoped to close in on the border by late morning. Sheds dotted the landscape where tobacco leaves, the king crop in this area, were hung up to dry and cure.

Along the way, we crossed paths with a man selling tanned hides and furs. Stopping for a rest and to look at his furs, I obviously showed way too much interest in a particularly beautiful sheepskin with long white wool. It was just my luck to make small talk with a man who could probably sell ice to an Eskimo. I had been seeking a possible souvenir before leaving Canada, but our money was already running low, so this was not a smart move. This guy—knowing fertile ground when he saw it—planted the seed, and just like that, I became the owner of a large, tanned sheepskin. To seal the deal, he assured me that I could ship it home from the post office just ten miles down the road. I strapped the skin—the size of a large sleeping bag when rolled up—onto my bike, and we hit the road. Imagine my surprise upon arriving at the post office to find out my fur buddy had left out the small detail that Canada had just begun a postal strike and that the sheepskin would remain a fixture on my bike.

As we once again prepared to leave Canada, I thought about the contrast between those first early days of our trip in British Columbia to 3,000 miles later in Ontario. The countryside was certainly different, as was the weather, but the biggest contrast existed within ourselves. Our appearances were certainly different. We started out looking a bit pale compared to our now seasoned and weathered faces. Our gear no longer had that neat, like-new look but rather portrayed that *rode hard* look. Over the miles, I—being kind of a packrat—had acquired a number of objects found on the roadway, such as a length of rope, a small tarp, and a couple of tools. Unlike my neatly packed bicycle from the early days of the trip, various items now hung from my bike, along with a sheepskin that gave me the appearance of a hoarder on wheels.

But the largest contrast was with how I saw things. This travel made me look at people from a perspective much deeper than first impressions. From the people we encountered who had very little yet gave us so much, to the people who never gave us a second glance, to the folks who wanted to hear and share every detail of our trip, this was a ride of contrasts. And I realized that this is the case wherever you go. On any given day of our trip, how I saw or chose to look at things determined what I took with me. When we encountered a large hill to climb, was it an obstacle in our way, or was it an opportunity leading to a great downhill on the backside? Was the perfect tailwind more perfect due to the previous day's strong headwind? Would the sun on our faces have felt nearly so good if it hadn't been preceded by three days of rain?

Every day, we were getting closer to the trip end, but I felt certain that these experiences would be carried with me and not forgotten. I no longer needed to remind myself what this trip was about. The destination would certainly arrive, but I felt even then that the journey would continue.

CHAPTER 13

Great Lakes and Friends

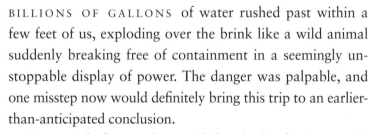

BILLIONS OF GALLONS of water rushed past within a few feet of us, exploding over the brink like a wild animal suddenly breaking free of containment in a seemingly unstoppable display of power. The danger was palpable, and one misstep now would definitely bring this trip to an earlier-than-anticipated conclusion.

Fortunately for us, along with hundreds of other people perched on the safe side of a fenced observation area at Niagara Falls, we were in no danger unless we did something stupid. Not that stupid things hadn't happened here in the past. More than one person attempted to go over the falls in everything from barrels to inner tubes. Compared to these antics, biking across the country with thousands of cars flying by within inches of us made us seem like cautious geniuses.

Niagara Falls, like the Grand Canyon or Old Faithful, jumps to the forefront of natural attractions for most Americans. As we completed our trek across Ontario, the falls was our portal back into the United States. All natural wonders evoke images in our minds that, upon actually visiting, may not live up to our expectations. Like a young guy in high school with over-the-top expectations of what prom night might bring, the reality at the end of the night might very well be less than what was hoped for. For me, Niagara Falls was like prom night.

Don't get me wrong, Niagara Falls is worth the trip. Broken into two channels, the Niagara River runs through two countries and forms the American Falls and the Canadian "Horseshoe" Falls. The sheer volume and power of the flowing water culminating in a spectacular cascade of almost 200 feet is truly mesmerizing, with tourists drawn to the observation platforms like kids to a circus tent. Over a half million gallons of water *per second* blow over the brink of the falls to create this display of nature.

It was also a disappointment, at least for me. Niagara Falls is not unlike a circus lion that is promoted as the king of beasts but is in fact a trained and contained shadow of its wild brethren. Niagara Falls, which before man intervened must have been unimaginable, is today a tamed beast, harnessed for its power and garishly displayed. In 1969, the water to the American Falls was actually "shut off," to consider removing loose rock at the bottom to create a more spectacular view. A sad, unnatural sort of geologic facelift.

I guess my prom night was not all that I had hoped for, but as we rode off into Buffalo, New York, I reminded myself that nature always wins in the end, eventually. It might take another millennia or longer, but someday the mighty Niagara

River will again flow free and unimpeded as the cycle of evolution continues.

We biked right through an old downtown part of Buffalo, which felt like a large, deserted city. With hardly a car to be seen and litter blowing down the streets, we felt like some of the last people on earth. On the heels of the circus atmosphere of Niagara Falls we had just left, this was another shock to our systems, especially as to how quickly the scenery can change, even on a bicycle. All I had ever heard about Buffalo, New York, was about the gazillion feet of snow they get every year. Granted we were riding through in August, but we weren't taking any chances so we cranked up the pedal revolutions and got out of town. We left on Highway 18, and tied into the Parkway Ride along the southern shore of Lake Ontario. This four-lane highway heading east and west closely followed the contours of the shoreline, making for one of the most beautiful rides of our trip. A four-lane highway hardly sounds like the ideal path for a bicycle ride, but this was different. Because the primary four-laners between Rochester and Canada were either Highway 104 or I-90, Highway 18 was left as a scenic drive, virtually untraveled. I noted in my journal that, in 30 miles, we saw a grand total of four cars traveling in either direction. As proof, I had Denise snap a picture of me and my bike lying on the white stripe down the middle of the two eastbound lanes.

Daylight started to fade into a windless evening, and the sun set over Lake Ontario, the lake like a pane of glass. We felt completely welcomed back to the United States as we rolled up to Golden Hill State Park on the lakeshore. As we prepared and ate a meal of tacos, the sun dipped into the lake, and we enjoyed as tranquil and peaceful a spot as we had stayed thus far. The slight inconvenience of a broken spoke earlier in the afternoon, and the disappointment of the Niagara Falls circus was offset by a great night's rest on the added comfort of a thick, cushy sheepskin on top of my camp pad. Life was good.

WAKING EARLY IN the morning and with Denise still sound asleep, I took the opportunity to walk the shoreline. Having grown up on Lake Winnebago in Wisconsin, a large lake itself, I was reminded of so many mornings as a kid. I truly loved the countless hours I had spent enjoying the lake in equally countless ways. Even as a youngster of 5 or 6, I had walked the shorelines. Most days, to my mother's chagrin yet endless patience, I had returned home with pocketsful of shells, stones, and a collection of bugs, night crawlers, or whatever else. I had occasionally found something of interest that had washed ashore with the large waves from the east. I would look across ten miles of restless lake, wondering from where on that far distant shore the item had come. By age 8, I had been allowed to take out the old rowboat my father had built. Back then, I rode crests of waves, exploring and creating my own daily adventures.

With Lake Ontario alive in the earliest light of that morning and a building breeze creating nervous ripples, I realized I was living out some of my earliest dreams spawned on the shores of Lake Winnebago. Soon, I'd be face to face again with everyday life, but I knew without a doubt that I would find ways to always keep dreams and adventures close by.

On the Midwestern leg of the trip, Bill Rue from the *Oshkosh Daily Northwestern* had interviewed Denise and I when we had passed through Oshkosh, Wisconsin. After the interview, we had been talking about the trip when Bill observed, "You know, there are probably a bunch of people who can't even imagine a trip like this, but there are probably many thousands who have a dream but never pursue it. Of those many thousands, a few thousand, maybe, start to roughly plan and talk it out but never get it started. Of those few thousand, maybe a hundred actually get a start and of those hundred, perhaps a handful see it through."

Having never really thought about it in that way, I realized he was probably right and asked, "Why is that?"

"Life," he replied. "Most people have dreams, particularly when they're younger. Next thing you know, along comes a car payment, mortgage, family, etc., and before you know it the dream, while maybe not dead, is buried."

Walking back to our campsite, I remembered this conversation and imagined how difficult it could be to keep dreams alive. I realized that it might be difficult, if not impossible, to experience things like this trip in the future unless, like some, I chose to forego the things like cars, homes, and family. Although this worked for some, I realized it would not be for me. Like so much of this trip, my challenge in life would be finding a balance between security and adventure.

When I arrived back at camp, I found Denise up and at it, as was so often the case. I had been gone longer than I thought, and she already had the bags packed, the tent down, and although we were out of food, the hot chocolate ready. Denise was a worker, plain and simple, and to top it off, she did the work without trying to make me feel guilty. Despite this, I couldn't help but wonder when she would ask to redeem all those guilt points like a frequent flier cashing in air miles. I knew she had banked a daunting mountain of credits, and I had visions of endless days of payback.

With cups of hot chocolate for fuel and the return of our friends the tailwinds, we headed out onto the Parkway by ourselves, once again alone on a four-lane highway. After a couple of effortless hours of being blown along and running on hot chocolate sugar fumes, we cut off the Parkway to the town of Hamlin, New York, where we found a grocery and chowed down on a sidewalk bench.

Finishing our street-side meal, we jumped onto Highway 18, which we thought would take us back onto the Parkway. Instead, within a short time, we found ourselves cruising into downtown Rochester. Despite maneuvering through the noontime rush-hour traffic and noise, I was still able to hear that familiar high-pitched *ping* as a spoke let go on my bike. As I rolled to a stop, I noted that the broken spoke was once again on the freewheel side, meaning I'd have to break out the freewheel tool and adjustable wrench that I hadn't thought of since outside of Williston, North Dakota, where I had to approach a crew of oil rig roughnecks to borrow a wrench while wearing biking shorts. This time, as if the broken spoke were not enough to deal with, I realized the jaws on the adjustable wrench had broken, leaving me with no way to loosen the tight nut on the freewheel.

As hundreds of noon-hour cars rushed past, I once again had to seek the help of strangers, dressed the same as in Williston. I knocked at the first door, and was met by a child of about 10. He took one look at me wearing my biking outfit and a week's worth of whiskers, and I could tell he was remembering everything his parents had taught him about scary-looking strangers. As he slammed and dead-bolted the door, I surmised that I needed to look elsewhere.

Two more doors down, an elderly gentleman came to the door and, without judging my appearance, listened to my sad story and offered the use of his tools. As Denise and I wheeled our bikes up the driveway to the garage, Pete met us with two glasses of ice-cold lemonade. He handed me an old, heavy pipe wrench, apologizing that it was all he had. As I replied that beggars can't be choosers, the nut broke loose from the extra weight and leverage of the big wrench.

While we worked on the bike and talked with Pete, we learned that he was retired from the Kodak camera company. He and his wife had lived in Rochester their entire lives. When I asked if his wife was inside, I sensed a distracted response. He nodded, but began to explain that his wife had been ill for some time, and that her doctors expected her to pass on soon. Tears rolled down his face as he spoke, and we told him how sorry we were and apologized for our intrusion. With a hand on my arm, he said that this brief break was what he had needed, and he wished us well.

Before heading back inside to his wife, he insisted that I keep the wrench, in case the same problem arose again. I slipped the several-pound wrench into my pack—for once not considering the weight, but rather feeling gratitude that comes only from a stranger's gift. Despite his own difficult times, he cared enough to help us.

We shared a final handshake, and I could see in his eyes memories of days when he and his wife were young and starting their dreams. I hoped that our presence had given him a brief respite from his grief and brought thoughts of happier days. As we started down the road, acid rain began to fall again. I couldn't say for sure whether this was the cause of the sting in my eyes or if it was due to riding into, and now out of, Pete's life.

WE CONTINUED ALONG the southern shore of Lake Ontario and a few miles inland on Highway 18. After we passed the east end of the lake, we began to cut across New York, headed for Vermont. We found ourselves passing through small communities almost every five miles, as opposed to legs in the Northwest where we would bike 40 miles or more without ever passing a town. Although this caused us a bit more grief in dealing with the increased traffic, I found I preferred hitting these small towns rather than planning a route to miss them. We appreciated that the people throughout these communities slowed down as they approached bikers and took the time to wave to strangers.

I found it interesting to consider the differing travel philosophies people have regarding trips of this nature. Some folks expressed a preference to avoid people and issues of biking through communities as they traveled along. Denise and I seemed the opposite. Although we both really enjoyed time spent on little-traveled mountain roads and passes or along miles of remote forest or open prairie, our interactions with the people who inhabited the land had been most enjoyable and interesting to us. As we pedaled through varied territory, the good, the bad, and the ugly had all entered our lives. Although we would have chosen to avoid some of these encounters at the time, when looking back, we realized that each contributed to making our trip complete.

If we had stayed in motels every night, eaten all meals at restaurants, and never mingled with the locals, our travel style would have had little more significance than an air flight, train passage, or car travel. Although the scenery was beautiful, I believed the land was defined by the people who had made their lives there. Traveling as we were, we interacted with these people in their daily lives, in a very personal sense as opposed to the commercial style you might experience in a restaurant or motel. Although our visits and stays were brief, we continued to be amazed with how people reached out to us and how we became, however briefly, involved in their lives.

Passing through a small community called Pultneyville, I was struck that although the 1980s generation now inhabited it, the town felt as if its history had been preserved. The road and countryside were beautiful, with farms, homes, and businesses that evidenced the centuries-old history of settlement sprinkled along the way. We often found ourselves passing old cemeteries or graveyards, with smoothly weathered stones with faded names that matched those on mailboxes we passed.

I found myself wondering how those from the past might judge those of the present. I remembered a poem called "The Calf Path" by Sam Walter Foss (1858–1911). In it, he traces the earliest meanderings of a calf through the countryside, and its meanderings eventually become the course of modern-day travel. The direction of our lives and the choices we make parallel the meanderings of the calf. Over the course of our trip, I time and again thought about the routes we traveled, probably as often as I wondered about the routes I have chosen and would choose for my life. Life, like travel, seldom follows the path "the crow flies." And like in life, we had to remind ourselves along the way that the routes we choose are less important than the experiences along those routes. We often found ourselves on "The Calf Path," both literally and figuratively, as we chose this mode of transportation across the country. Foss notes in his poem:

> *For men are prone to go it blind*
> *Along the calf-paths of the mind,*

And work away from sun to sun
To do what other men have done.
They follow in the beaten track,
And out and in, and forth and back,
And still their devious course pursue,
To keep the path that others do.

Foss seemed to chide us for foolishly not changing and adapting with the times. Despite this, I always hoped we'd find room to follow some old paths or variations of, as we had done. There was certainly a time and place for following direct routes, but there are important reasons for sometimes following the back roads. Although longer and often bumpy, they helped us feel the soul of the land that couldn't be experienced at 70 miles an hour on 10 inches of concrete.

Just five miles out of Pultneyville, we found ourselves biking past a beautiful old farmhouse nestled in a peach tree orchard. Noticing an elderly woman tending to flower gardens, we pulled up to introduce ourselves and inquire if we might be allowed to camp for the night in the orchard. Brushing the dirt from her pants, Mrs. Brownell graciously invited us to set up our tent next to the barn on the edge of the peach grove. Walking us through knee-high grass, she showed us to a place protected from the wind by an ancient-looking barn. She told us that the farm had been in her family for generations. The barn, a masterpiece, had been built in 1846, by craftsmen with the simple hand tools of the time. At the time we passed through, it was 135 years old, standing strong on a sturdy foundation of round field-stone. Many of the sideboards were 18 inches wide and running many feet in length, hewn from large trees long since logged out.

The peach orchard itself was also well established. The trees had sturdy trunks and well-pruned branches reaching out wide and high, laden with a heavy crop of ripening fruit. Mrs. Brownell explained that she had lived there alone since her husband had passed on, and said that her son Tom and his family were visiting from Ohio. She then invited us to join them in her home later for fresh homemade peach cobbler. We thanked her for the hospitality and definitely accepted her invitation, and then got busy setting up our tent.

From where we stood on a hill by the barn, it was possible to look out over the orchard and to Lake Ontario on the horizon. I couldn't help but compare this day to one earlier in our trip, when we camped in the cherry orchard in Osoyoos, British Columbia. There, too, we sat on a hillside with soft grass cushioning our sleeping bags as we looked out over acres of cherry trees on the shores of a lake.

Just when we had almost finished, a boy of about 10 bounded up to check out our camp. With shyness not being an issue, he introduced himself as Nathan, the grandson of Mrs. Brownell. He had been sent to fetch us for dessert, but he first wanted to know if we wanted to see him climb a peach tree. Not a stranger to tree climbing as a youngster myself, I have to say that Nate, with the fearlessness of youth, put me to shame. Before I could even reply, he was already partially up the trunk, scrambling from limb to limb until he literally stood atop the very highest branches about 15 feet up. We snapped a quick picture of the King of the Tree, and I was relieved when he descended just as quickly. He asked if I wanted to race him up a tree, and I quickly explained that I would love to but we really shouldn't keep his grandma and folks waiting. He looked at me with far more perception than I thought a 10-year-old was capable, and I realized he had my number, but he shrugged it off and led us to the farmhouse.

After introductions all around, we sat at a beautiful old dining table and were treated to warm-from-the-oven peach cobbler with vanilla ice cream. As laughter and conversation flowed around the table, Denise and I both felt almost a part of this wonderful family. Nathan's father Tom and I visited, and Tom explained that his mother was starting to have a few problems living alone. He didn't know how much longer she would be able to stay there on her own. It was easy to see the emotions that pulled at Tom, because he knew the time was coming when some difficult decisions would need to be made. I felt sorry for all of them as this chapter in their lives unfolded, as it does for all families at some point. This night, however, was a good time that I hoped we would all remember and treasure—I know we would. Thanking the Brownells for their generosity, we said our goodnights and good-byes, explaining that we intended to start early the next morning. As the moon shone over the orchard on the shores of Lake Ontario, we zipped our tent shut for the night, closing out one of those days that made us wish our trip would never end.

KNOWING THAT WE were probably in the last week of our trip really brought us mixed emotions. Nights like the one with the Brownells made up for all the broken spoke–type days. At the same time, we also realized that we'd been on the road almost two months at this point, and we both had unfinished business and life waiting. In my case, I had my last year of school, plus student teaching and then searching for my first teaching position.

When I talked with people about going into education and teaching for a career, I found it interesting how many times I would hear, "Oh, you just want to have summer and all those holidays off!" It usually seemed to be said in a manner that insinuated that I should be apologetic. After having done this trip, I had to admit that I sure wouldn't be pained to know I'd have time off to pursue other dreams. Prior to returning to college to become a teacher, I had worked as a golf course greenskeeper, where working 60- to 65-hour weeks in summer was the norm. Although I enjoyed the work, I could see my life was out of balance, with neither the time nor energy to pursue the adventures I dreamed about.

When I had decided to quit my job and return to school, it was with some apprehension, but I had no doubt I had made the right decision. Education would certainly not be an easy career, but it would be a very rewarding one. Not only would I receive personal satisfaction, but I would also be able to teach lessons that I had learned and consider valuable, such as leading a fulfilling lifestyle. Having a rewarding career is important just as is a personal life. Balance between the two is the goal and the challenge.

As we headed down Highway 370 toward Rome, New York, we left Lake Ontario behind. This road had light travel due to I-90 being just south of us. The freeway absorbed all the traffic in a hurry to get from here to there. As we neared Rome, we felt pretty good and decided to put on a few more miles.

Later in the afternoon, the sky began to take on that heavy, pewter gray look that usually precedes a thunderstorm. Not wanting to take on lightning, we pulled up at a farmhouse near a small town called Holland Patent, and received permission to camp for the night. We had traveled 103 miles for the day and were ready to stop, thunderstorm or not. As the sky darkened, we felt a definite urgency to prepare our food quickly. We had just finished cleaning our dishes when a sudden powerful gust billowed our tent and chased us inside. With the first raindrops following us, we zippered the door and tried to sleep as all hell let loose in wind, rain, and lightning for most of the evening. Long since wise to setting up our tent on high ground and placing a good ground cloth under us, we weathered a doozy of a storm. It always amazed me how safe and secure I could feel behind nylon fabric as nature let loose on the other side of it. Less-than-a-sixteenth-inch-thick fabric allowed me a good night's sleep, despite several nearby lightning strikes and accompanying ground-shaking booms.

WHILE THE STORM pounded away outside our tent, I took some time to look back in my journal. Prior to the start of this trip, I knew it would be important to keep a daily record of our trip. I also kept a journal the previous summer while biking from Florida to Wisconsin with Steve. Over the following years, I was able to relive a bit about our days, the incidents, and the people we met during that two weeks. As time passed, details were easily forgotten, but just a word, description, or name can trigger a flood of memories.

Many times on that southern trip, I had been dog-tired after long-mileage days in extreme heat, and often was tempted to skip journaling for the day. I thought that if I did that once, it would be a slippery slope to not journaling at all, and I didn't want to let that happen. Steve had also started a journal on the Florida trip but had let it go early on, and didn't have much to look back on in the end. I knew that these trips would be adventures of a lifetime. I was certain that 10, 20, or more years down the road, they would be more meaningful than ever. I pictured myself looking back on these days of my life, and in some cases not believing what we had done. I also saw myself sharing these adventures with kids of my own, maybe igniting a spark in them like my father had with me.

Denise had also started her own journal on the trip, but I'm pretty sure that she took one break for a day, which led to another and ended there. I wish she had continued her own recordings, because personal perspectives are always somewhat different. I would have enjoyed comparing our different thoughts of the same situations.

As I journeyed back through the pages, it was easy to relive the days and experiences not only through the written words, but also by their appearance. My earliest days of writing were neat and concise, just as Sister Mary Arthur had drilled into my head in fourth grade at St. Mary's Catholic School. As the trip rolled on and days became long or rest stops short, the quality of my penmanship told its own tale of how the day went. Although I recorded the day's weather in writing, it was also somewhat evident in the sometimes smeared writing caused by raindrops. Mealtime menus, always important footnotes in any day on the road, were also occasionally indicated by splotches of ketchup or grease marks on a page.

Through these pages were names of short-time friendships. Some would endure a lifetime, and others would soon be a memory. Either way, each person played a part in this journey that would live on for me through my journal and maybe for others through this account.

WHEN WE EMERGED in the morning, the sky was clear and the sun was back in charge. Happy to see we had survived the night, our elderly hosts invited us in for breakfast. Although we were appreciative, the meal was served with a lengthy helping of descriptions of the wife's recent gall bladder surgery. We rushed through the meal, chasing down our scrambled eggs that were a little too runny with surgery details. We expressed our gratitude, and made a somewhat hasty departure. Later in the day, I made a note in my journal, a reminder to my older self to spare people—particularly much younger people—from details of any operations I have.

AS WE CUT through Upstate New York, the morning started out promising, and we had anticipated entering into Vermont by perhaps the end of the day. The air had that clean freshness that follows a heavy rainstorm. With a beautiful sunrise, we rolled through a winding roadway bordered by mature hardwood trees whose limbs reached out and formed a canopy over the roadway in places, and passed a man driving a beautiful thoroughbred gelding hitched to a restored carriage.

A short time later, however, our previously sunny skies began to cloud over, the temperature dipped, and the road began to buckle with numerous hills as the first drops of rain began to fall. Once again, the worm had turned, and the day that had started out encouraging was becoming challenging. We pulled on our raingear and soldiered on over the now silver, wet roadway, until the clouds really opened up. With the rain too heavy to continue, we pulled off the road and ducked into a small antique and gift store called The Acorn Shoppe. We were happy to have found shelter in an interesting place where we could pass the time, and we also met Hector, the owner, who welcomed us to browse around. After learning about our trip, he invited us to have lunch with his family in his home in the back of the store. Serving us grilled cheese sandwiches, hot cider, and salad, and topping that off with warm elderberry pie, Hector didn't realize how close he came to having long-term guests.

Fortunately for our hosts, the skies cleared as we enjoyed our lunch. With thanks and dry clothes, we were back on Highway 29, headed toward Saratoga Springs, New York. Although the rain had stopped and the roadway had leveled and improved, the traffic worsened as we skirted the Adirondack Mountains. We learned that Saratoga Springs is home to the oldest thoroughbred horse-racing track in the United States, and it appeared we were passing through as everyone was headed there to take one last shot on the ponies, as it was the last day of the race season.

As often seemed to be the case in Upstate New York, the transition from countryside to city was very abrupt, with Saratoga Springs being no exception. In this case, we were biking along a roadside in the country one minute, and suddenly had entered the city—as abruptly as the Yellow Brick Road ended at the Emerald City for Dorothy and company. In our case, however, the section of Saratoga Springs we entered was no Emerald City. We found ourselves in an old, dilapidated section of town that had definitely seen better days. As we biked past abandoned cars on a potholed road, we were obviously catching the attention of some street characters who were not looking to offer us the hospitality we had enjoyed with Hector and his family earlier in the day.

Both Denise and I were on alert, the hair on the back of our necks standing. This was not a great place to be in a car, much less on bicycles. As we upped our speed, we noticed a traffic light ahead that was probably going to stop us. Just as we had decided that, red or not, we weren't about to stop around here, an angel in the form of a New York State Patroller pulled alongside us, and although no words were spoken, he signaled for us to ride off his back bumper. In this manner, we passed safely and quickly through the next blocks until we were in a better part of town.

We made it through the seedy side of town, but we had other issues with which to deal. The traffic was still heavy as cars rolled toward the racetrack, and the daylight was quickly fading. We found ourselves rushing through the residential area of town, not wanting to spend the evening in the city and not feeling too sure about finding a place even if we wanted to. After riding out of the city's east side, we again transitioned quickly from city to country and found ourselves in a large swampy area with no prospects for campsites. By this time, it was getting dark, the road was narrow, and both of us were more than ready to call it a day. We pulled to a stop and tried to come up with a plan. Even in the fading light, I saw a tired, desperate look on Denise's face that matched identically what I was feeling. With no other option but to ride on in the dark, we did so for another couple of miles, with only one weak light to guide both of us. As cars continued to pass by on their way into the city, we felt hemmed in by the black of night and vulnerable as bright headlights blinded us. Despite our limited ability to see our surroundings, we knew swamp bounded us on either side of the road. After 2,000 miles of fairly open country in the first part of the trip, we hadn't adjusted very well to the increased traffic and population that became more prevalent as we traveled further east.

Just when we felt we were without options, the faint glow of a light was visible about a mile up the road. Hoping for the best, we covered the distance quickly with that reserve energy one draws on when the chips are down. The light turned out to be in the yard of a nice home set back in the trees. We debated approaching the house and asking permission to camp for the evening. We knew, however, that any knock on the door at night in the country, particularly with no car visible in the driveway, might set off some warning bells for the occupants. With our only other choice to continue down the dark road to who knew where, we took our chances, leaving our bikes exposed in the beam of the yard light as we approached the front door. As we knocked, we had some of the same trepidation as a hitchhiker hoping for a ride but unsure of who might pull over or of their intentions. We were lucky when a 40-ish woman, flanked by what looked to be her 20-something son, answered the door.

Following our plan, Denise did the talking. We figured she would appear less threatening.

"Hello, we're really, really sorry to bother you, but we are on a bike trip across the country, and tonight we got caught in the dark. We wondered if you would possibly allow us to set up our tent for the night?"

"Oh, my," the woman said, "I was startled when I heard the knock at the door and hadn't heard a car drive up."

I repeated, "We're really, really sorry," as I professed my genuine mea culpas. "I know, I would feel the same way. It's just that we didn't have any idea of what else to do, and we had to give this a shot."

Looking over her shoulder at her son, she summed up our appearance with, "I guess they don't look very dangerous to me, Brian," she said with a smile. "What do you think?"

Brian, a rather husky young man, swung the door open and said, "I think we should get them inside before the mosquitoes eat them alive," picking up on a very real concern of mine during the last couple of swamp miles.

Once again, in a brief period of minutes, potential disaster was transformed into deliverance. Setting up our tent next to their glorious in-ground heated swimming pool, we even had a chance for a quick dip before the family, now joined by the dad, came back to visit and bring sandwiches and a six-pack of ice-cold Iron City beer. Steve, the dad, had just come home from work, and I'm sure must have questioned his wife's and son's willingness to invite strangers onto their property in the middle of the night.

It wasn't long, however, before we were again sharing stories of our trip—by now well over 3,000 miles long—and fielding the usual questions. Margee and her son Brian were inclined to view our trip as almost impossible to believe, expressing doubts that they would ever try anything like it. Steve, however, reveled in our descriptions of the places we'd been and repeatedly uttered wishes to do something similar.

The sandwiches and six-pack were soon gone, and the mosquitoes were getting hungrier by the minute. We called it a night after profusely thanking our hosts for their kindness on what had been a desperate evening for us. Knowing the morning would bring an early departure, we said our good-byes, and then zipped ourselves in for the night, once again "safe and secure" as we contemplated crossing the state line into Vermont the following morning. New York had been quite a state, both in time and experiences. We drifted to sleep knowing we probably only had a few more days on the road before reaching the Atlantic Ocean.

CHAPTER 14

Closing In

THE TRANQUILITY OF the quiet morning air erupted with vicious, heart-stopping growling and snarling. As Denise ran to get back on her bike, which I was holding, an enormous Rottweiler came flying around the corner of a nearby auto body shop. Once Denise landed on her bike, we tore off down the road, escaping Rover, who obviously wanted more than a game of fetch. Talk about *meaner than a junkyard dog!*

During our training rides back in the Midwest, we had become accustomed to being chased by farm dogs. Interestingly, this was the first and only time on the entire trip that we had a run-in with, in this case, man's *worst* friend. Following our trip and a recounting of this tale, Denise was asked if she thought she could have outrun the beast. Her reply spoke volumes. "I didn't have to, I only had to outrun Bob." That's my girl!

With an early-morning *adios* to New York and a *hello* to Vermont, we had only moments earlier crossed the state line on a back road that didn't even offer the typical "Welcome to

_____" sign seen in most states. I guess the angry pooch would have to suffice as our "Welcome Wagon" hostess. In a short time, Vermont lived up to its image of a scenic landscape. As scenic as it was, however, the bucolic countryside provided its own wake-up call as we proceeded on Highway 11, and quickly found ourselves using our gears, as we began climbing the steep gradient of the Green Mountains. The trees hemmed us in tightly as we wound our way up the narrow old road, and we frequently found ourselves standing in our pedals as we cranked up a particularly steep section. From time to time, we rolled past isolated homes nestled back in the trees, and we occasionally crossed paths with local folks who seemed to fit the stereotype of earthy, down-home people. I suspected this reputation of backwoods slow living attracts and holds a certain type of people looking for that lifestyle.

I noticed that the steep hills tuckered me out quickly if I didn't pace myself. With the end of the trip nearing, Denise and I both noticed that we had been pushing the pace more than usual. I guess that "finish line in sight" mentality had kicked in, and we found ourselves torn between wanting to finish, and not wanting the trip to end.

Having pushed a bit hard through the hills, we were looking for a reason to take a break, and we didn't have to look long. We noticed a number of small signs along the roadway in front of homes that advertised local arts and crafts. As we made our way across the state, we discovered numerous small, out-of–the-home businesses advertising items for sale, including colorful quilts, elaborate weather vanes, and personalized wooden signs. If I were in the market for hand-woven baskets or rugs, I could choose to shop from quite a few places. And if I were a lonely pancake looking to be made complete with some homemade maple syrup, then Vermont was the place to be. These items and much more were evidence of the artists who call Vermont home.

As we continued, we saw long, broad planks of wood leaning against an old wood barn. We pulled off the road, where we met Gunnar, the owner of the property. Gunnar could best be described as a guy who looked like he came of age near the end of the heyday for hippies. He was probably about 30 or so, with an "it's cool, be happy" demeanor. As he showed us around, he explained his business. He custom-cut enormous planks with a huge, old circular saw to create unique tabletops for customers who then had the custom table base and legs built. Even though Gunnar was one heck of a salesman, I was safe, namely because (1) I did not have any money, (2) my bike was already too loaded with my sheepskin, and (3) where would I even put a table without a home at this point? Gunnar invited us into his lair and showed us what might have been his backup income to the tabletops. He pulled out a one-gallon resealable storage bag. He never said it was pot, but I don't think he was offering us oregano. When we declined, he became a little more stand-offish. We assured him though that we weren't DEA agents, and that his secret was safe with us. With a hand slap and a "be cool, man" from Gunnar, we were back on our way.

Not much further down the road, we had another opportunity for a brief rest after we biked through a heavily
forested, hilly area. When I looked off to my right into the
woods, I thought my eyes were playing tricks on me. There,
about a hundred feet or so into the woods, sat a huge old
wooden boat—not quite a ship, but not a mere fishing skiff.
This vessel was approximately 50 feet long, with a beam of
about 12 feet and a depth of 5 feet. Made completely of
wood, the boat had the appearance of an old fishing launch
with a swept-up bow and large open center area. This was a
boat that would have been used in the big waters of the Great
Lakes or along the ocean coast—neither of which was anywhere near. Also, this boat had been at home there for a long
time: The 50-plus-year-old trees that grew closely around it
were evidence that it had not recently been left here. As I
walked around its stern and up its starboard side, I wondered
about its history and the life of who had left it behind. Like so
many things scattered and abandoned across the country, this
boat had once represented someone's big dreams. Had this
craft ever seen the water, and if so, where? How did it come
to be abandoned here decades ago, far from any big water?
What became of the owner and his dreams? Not able to find
anyone in the near vicinity, we rode on once again, leaving a
mystery behind that in some ways was probably more comfortable than the answers.

With 85 miles in for the day, we rolled into Springfield,
Vermont, at the eastern edge of the narrowest part of the
state. We decided to make camp there so that we could spend

at least one night in Vermont. We also planned to camp one night in New Hampshire, where we would be the next day. At this location, Vermont and New Hampshire, when combined, were only about 100 miles across total, and we could have easily traveled from New York and made camp in Maine, thus riding within four states in one day. Why I thought this was important or why I even noted it in my journal escapes me, so perhaps I had just been on the road too long.

Being late in the day, we ate a quick meal at a McDonald's before we struck out to find a campsite. Once again, we had waited too late, and the best we could find was a spot behind a ball field in town. The local police checked us out and then gave us the okay; however, the spot proved to be noisy, bright with lights, and perhaps worst of all, a popular hangout for teens. We passed a restless night in the glow of lights, listening to the sounds of traffic and teens laughing and being teens. I contemplated how this less-than-ideal campsite was a far cry from the quiet camps in Glacier National Park or Clark Fork, Idaho, and also realized that the following night might be our last night camping on this trip.

HAPPY TO MAKE an early departure the following morning, we stopped at the same McDonald's down the road and shared a basic breakfast. Our funds were really low at this point, and we were uncertain whether our dollars would hold out as we closed in on Maine. Once we got to the end of the trip, I would have no problem borrowing a few bucks from my dad who was meeting us, but we were at the bottom of the barrel for the time being, with two big days of biking still ahead.

I'd have given anything at that point to convert that sheepskin back into money. Two days of biking represented a lot of calories for two people. With only a total of about six dollars left between the two of us, we had a couple of hungry days ahead. Down the road, we hoped to find good careers with decent paydays, and I was sure having to scrimp would contribute to the memories of this trip in later years.

WITH AN EARLY start out of Vermont that morning, we crossed into New Hampshire, winding our way over a variety of back roads toward Concord. Just down the road, we found ourselves in a town named Rochester for the second time in a week, but this time it was on the western border of New Hampshire. Unlike in Rochester, New York, I didn't have to deal with any broken spokes, the road was fine, and traffic was nonexistent. And because we were getting further along into summer and were so far north, we were starting to experience the shorter daylight hours as well as some cooler mornings.

As we neared Rochester by midday, our appetites were roaring. We both almost stopped dead in the road when the smell of barbecuing chicken wafted across our path. Our noses led us to a church just up the road that was sponsoring a chicken roast as a fundraiser. Unfortunately, we would have used all of our remaining money to ante up the $5.25 needed for one dinner. With a day and a half to ride, we just couldn't afford it.

So many times during our trip, we had been the fortunate recipients of kindness, invited to join as guests for meals. Now, in our somewhat ragged trip gear and looking a bit worse for wear, we didn't exactly blend in with these folks in their Sunday finest. Certainly not willing to beg our way in or be seen drooling, we hung out in the area for another 15 minutes, just to savor the rich aroma from the grills. We then hopped back on our bikes and settled for dreaming up what we were going to eat at the end of the trip. Like castaways on an island, we conjured up feasts with entrees, side dishes, and fabulous desserts in quantities more suited for entire families. Though spectacular in vision, these images provided little in locomotion.

After a day of riding 105 miles with a lot of hill climbing, and fueled only by fantasy calories, we found a welcome mat rolled out to us by the local fire department. A few firefighters invited us to set up our tent next to the firehouse, and offered to share their meal with us, which we very much appreciated. As we settled in for our last night on the road, I'm sure we each entertained our separate thoughts—not only of what we had done, but also of what we would do from here on.

Denise and I had met less than a year ago, and although our relationship extended beyond mere friendship, neither of us was really guessing what might happen down the stretch. One thing I knew for sure was that if the strength of a relationship was at all dependent on being able to confront and overcome adversity, then I was sharing a tent with someone of stronger willpower and determination than anyone I had known previously.

At that point in time, I think we both had more questions than answers, and they surely weren't going to be figured out that night. We both knew the coming year would probably sort things out. And we knew the next day would be one of the biggest of big days, so we called it a night. Thanks to our firemen buddies, we slept with full bellies and nary a stomach growl.

CHAPTER 15

The Homestretch

A CERTAIN ENERGY propels a person forward when on the homestretch of any endeavor. With over 3,600 miles behind us, we were like that freight train with momentum that made stopping difficult. Despite the weariness of months and miles, we broke camp with strength to spare and an eagerness to savor each of our remaining miles. Saying goodbye to our friends at the firehouse, we fueled up on fresh-baked goods and juice, and hit the road early for what promised to be a long day if, indeed, it was to be our last. In a matter of miles, we were greeted with "Welcome to Maine," as we headed for the coast down Highway 4. Although we knew the traffic would be heavy as we neared the coast and that we could avoid it by staying inland, we both agreed that we would ride alongside the ocean. After picking up Highway 111, we rode east to Highway 1, and with a briny sea breeze in our face, we pedaled the old coastal highway of Maine until we reached the rugged, irregular coast, where we had no choice but to travel north.

As expected, traffic had picked up, but with a decent shoulder to ride on and the exhilaration of the day propelling us, the morning's miles passed quickly, even as we found our way around and through Portland. The biking gods surely must have been smiling on us, or I would have broken a spoke in Portland as I did in every other major city. We set our sights on Freeport, Maine, the home of L.L. Bean, a manufacturer and retailer of clothes and gear for the outdoors. In an age before the Internet and World Wide Web, paper catalogs were still the origins of dreams and wishing. Having grown up thumbing the pages of their catalogs, I made wish lists in my mind for flannel-lined shirts, canvas brush pants, and a pair of their famous leather hunting boots. With literally only a few bucks left in our pockets, we knew our list items would remain wishes, but wishing and looking didn't cost anything, and today we intended to do just that.

As we pulled into Freeport at about noon, the traffic was indeed terrible. Because we had expected this, we were able to tolerate it easier. We jockeyed our bicycles, heavy with packs, through the busy streets, and drew more than a few stares from curious folks. Once at the large L.L. Bean retail store, we took our bikes up onto the front porch and, concerned for the security of our gear, leaned them right against the wall. We felt we should have received a commission from the company for looking a bit like a live advertisement for the outdoor adventure lifestyle.

After about 30 minutes of answering dozens of questions about our trip from people who approached us, we finally made our way into the store where I was ready to meet my catalog dreams. We wound our way through woolen socks, hats, leather gloves, and boots, and I began to feel the inevitable letdown that usually occurs when reality cannot possibly meet the fantasy of the mind. Just like models without makeup become like the girls next door, so too did my dream gear. Seeing it stacked in quantities on tables and shelves just like in any other store and absent the enticing catalog descriptions accompanying pictures definitely diminished my fantasy. Or at least that was what I told myself as I walked out of the store still coveting the gear of my dreams.

When I walked back outside, my dashed dreams quickly turned to nightmares as Denise and I stared at the now-empty spot where we had left our bikes. We ran left and right and around the corners of the building, hoping against all odds that our bikes had only been moved. They were nowhere in sight.

We stopped all who looked helpful, inquiring again and again whether anyone had seen our bikes, each time hearing the same unhelpful response. We could not believe that someone would steal our bikes and gear after almost 4,000 miles and within 50 miles of our trip destination—and right off the front porch of L.L. Bean in front of hundreds of people. I kicked myself for having been so stupid as to have left our bikes unlocked.

We continued to ask people, looking for help, looking for anything that might give us hope, until an elderly couple approached us. "Say, are you the cross-country bikers we heard about?" queried the old man.

Hardly in the mood to share trip stories, I somewhat rudely replied, "Almost cross-country. Someone just stole our bikes."

"Oh, I don't think anyone stole them, but I think someone is taking pictures of them down in the street," the woman replied, pointing toward the street out front.

We ran in the direction the woman indicated. Sure enough, there, two couples posed for pictures while straddling our bikes in the roadway. Wearing dress shirts and leather loafers, and with perfectly coiffed hair, dazzling smiles, and nary a drop of sweat, they didn't look like they even biked from the porch to the street, where they had taken our bikes.

Happy to have recovered our bikes, but pissed off enough that I was ready to make some dentist a windfall in smile repairs, I approached the couple. In the span of seconds, the four faux bicyclists managed to disarm both Denise and me as they gushed over us and our trip. They had overheard us discussing it with people on the front steps when we had first pulled up. They explained that they had no intent to steal our gear, and that they didn't think we would mind them posing with our bikes while we shopped. After hearing their innocent and seemingly genuine explanation, and their congratulations on completing our trip, we found ourselves—believe it or not—posing with them, sans the perfect hair and loafers on our part.

With this detour of excitement behind us and all we could take of the crowds of eager shoppers, we began riding out of Freeport, heading up Highway 1, each revolution of the pedals leading us closer to the end.

By 2:00 P.M., the morning donuts had long since been burned off. We pooled our remaining money, including change from the bottoms of our handlebar packs, for a grand total of $4.62. Heading into a grocery in Brunswick, Maine, we emerged with our final meal on the road—a pack of Double Stuf Oreos and a quart of chocolate milk. As we sat on a curb and munched away, we shared a laugh as we remembered that early-spring training ride from River Falls to Oshkosh, Wisconsin, when we had traveled on bread and water for two days after our money had been stolen.

This time, with plenty of sugar and little else, we hit the road, savoring the final 30 or so miles of our trip of a lifetime. The roadway once again veered in an eastward direction, and I noted with a smile on my face that our old friend Mariah the tailwind had joined us for a boost in those final miles. As the daylight began to fade, Denise and I made the final turn down a dead-end road leading to the home of Vera and Louis Mathieson, where my father stood in the street to greet us.

For almost the last time, we rolled to a stop; my dad grabbed my hand in his and, pulling me in, embraced me warmly—an infrequent occurrence—as he congratulated us. I found myself grateful for the fading light to hide the tear in my eye as I felt a strengthened bond with my father whose stories of war and adventure had inspired me. This time, I had given back to him.

After a day of riding 130 miles, contending with an almost trip-ending bicycle theft—all on limited food—we'd had enough for the day. We had just enough reserve energy to share a few stories, eat a quick meal, enjoy hot showers, and say good night. The following day, we would officially culminate the trip after biking the final hundred yards to the shoreline, where we would dip our wheels in the Atlantic Ocean.

AWAKENING FROM ONE of those sleeps of the dead, I was up early, looking forward to visiting with the Mathiesons and exploring the area. As expected, my father and Louis were already up and at the kitchen table, reliving their Navy seadog days and catching up on recent happenings.

Despite a thousand miles separating them, the two had remained best friends over the past 40 years, having forged an unbreakable bond, literally in the heat of battle on December 7, 1941. Both had served as machinist mates, maintaining and operating the massive engines on the battleship USS *Oklahoma* at Pearl Harbor. At the earliest signs of the Japanese attack that morning, they had both rushed to their battle stations. The *Oklahoma* had been perhaps the easiest target for the Japanese torpedo bombers and, within minutes of the attack, she had taken nine torpedoes in her side, causing her to capsize in a very short time.

My father, Louis, and a handful of other sailors had been trapped in the engine compartments three decks down when the hatches were dogged down. The ship had quickly begun to capsize. They knew that an air vent in the compartment led to topside and, with hopes of it being open, they knew that would be their only chance. In total darkness, they had boosted and pulled one another into the narrow, pitch black tunnel, pushing and pulling themselves along in the normally vertical shaft that had shifted horizontally as the ship rolled over. They discovered that the hatch had indeed been left open, but the air around them was filled with attacking planes, machine-gun fire and shrapnel. The water below was a burning, oily caldron. With no choice but to wish each other luck, they had jumped into the boiling mess.

Amid the action, neither had seen the other again that day. Later that night, after the immediate action of the day had passed, my father and Louis had been reunited in an outdoor area where they were receiving treatment for minor injuries they had incurred. While there, they both responded to a call for sailors to man ships headed out to sea to search for the Japanese task force that had launched the surprise attack. Both had reported for duty on a destroyer, the USS *Hull*. Louis had remained on the *Hull* for a short time before being shipped stateside due to a leg injury he had received on the day of the attack. The injury had become infected, and the doctors had initially wanted to amputate his leg. Fortunately, one doctor took exceptional care, allowing Louis to keep his leg. My father had remained on the *Hull* and fought in most of the frontline action until the *Hull* was sunk in Typhoon Cobra in December 1944. For three days and four nights, he and six other sailors attempted to survive in the ocean with no food or water. By a miracle, my father and three of the sailors had been rescued, but only after three others had been killed by sharks. Of the approximately 350 sailors originally aboard the *Hull*, only 55 had survived.

Louis and my father had not seen each other again during the war, but on September 5, 1951, Louis had heard a knock on his door and was surprised to see my father on the steps in his Navy uniform. Dad had been called back into active duty for the Korean War, and had been stationed on the East Coast at the time. Although they had stayed in touch by mail and theirs was a friendship forged for life, this had been their first time together in nine years. At the conclusion of our trip in 1981, I walked in the same doorway my father had entered in 1951, when he and Louis were reunited.

FROM THE START, I had known that Louis and Vera's would serve as the perfect ending point because they were just like family and their home stood right on the ocean. Denise and I had planned to dip our wheels into the Atlantic Ocean, concluding a journey that began by crossing the Arthur Laing Bridge leading off British Columbia's Sea Island in the Pacific Ocean.

Before we would do that though, Louis had made plans to take us on a boat ride to show us the area that reflected the rich history associated with the earliest settlers—in fact, Vera was a direct descendent of those on the *Mayflower*— and also out to an island to see a colony of puffins. Unfortunately, the wind was stiff and the ocean conditions were rough that morning, and Louis reminded me, "You know, you want to be careful getting in a boat with me and your dad. Our track record's not too good!"

With the boat ride on hold and Denise still sound asleep, I took a walk down to the ocean to have a look at where our trip would "officially" end. I walked the exposed rocks and drying kelp of low tide, with only the company of small skittering crabs about my feet. I contemplated the ocean and its significance on our coast-to-coast journey as well as the trip back to the Midwest the following day. My thoughts returned to summiting the last mountain in Montana and my first view of "Big Sky country" as we entered the plains. The ocean undoubtedly commanded the biggest of big skies as the horizon stretched into infinity. High above me a jet left its white contrail behind as it headed east through the blue sky. I thought about the flight at the start of our journey, when I looked down from 30,000 feet up and saw only a neat package of landscape below, unable to see or even imagine the many people, places, and experiences waiting for us. I wondered if someone was looking down from that jet at this moment, perhaps at the start of their own adventure, able to see only the coast and the ocean, oblivious of the myriad of lives and details unfolding below them. Certainly they hadn't a clue of my existence below them or of the details of what we had just completed. I felt strangely comfortable with the fact that I, and what we had just completed, stood there unseen and anonymous to those passing overhead.

I felt that with the completion of our trip, I had learned a secret, the details of which would carry me through a lifetime.

From far above, life below had been painted with a broad brush, but once we were on the road, we were immersed in the intimate details in our narrow sphere of travel. With a last glance upward at the passing jet, I smiled at the realization that we would now once again be part of the big picture as we slipped back into day-to-day life. Looking out at the ocean, I saw the curve of the earth meld together the sea and the sky; they became indistinguishable, yet each possessed a bounty of unique qualities and specific characteristics. As I was now about to continue with life as normal, I realized I was going back to being one of the crowd—indistinguishable but also unique, in part from our journey.

My musings were cut short by a yell from the road. I turned to see Steve waving at me. He had arrived in Owls Head only a few hours after us but had waited until morning to come to the house. He explained that his trip had been a good one, but that he was tired and ready to head home and back to work. Although our original plan of biking together hadn't ended up that way, Steve had enjoyed the folks he had met and the routes he had taken. We had no hard feelings between us because we all recognized early on that we had different agendas. Respecting these differences and making the necessary adjustments, we both moved forward. Steve is a great guy and, as I learned from our Florida trip, a tenacious biker. I was glad we had shared some elements of this trip, and I would always look back fondly at our incredible journey through the southern states in midsummer of 1980.

BACK AT THE house, Denise was up with news that a reporter from the local paper was stopping by to interview us about our trip. Having been interviewed several times, we felt we could offer a new perspective now that we had completed the trip. It was certainly different to be able to reflect back on its entirety as opposed to being partway through the journey. After rehashing stories and answering questions about the West Coast to Maine, we wrapped up the interview just in time for a feast of a lifetime—a lobster and clam bake, with the guests of honor fresh off the boats that morning. After our many questionable meals on the road, particularly the Double Stuf Oreos and our "fantasy meal" where we only inhaled the aroma of barbecued chicken due to lack of funds, this was the real deal. With bibs tied around our necks, we dug into a mountain of lobsters and consumed far more rich seafood than we should have.

Pushing away from the table with full bellies once again, we had one last duty of the day. Denise and I straddled our bikes and, happy for the short downhill ride to the ocean, we officially concluded our journey when our front tires entered the salty Atlantic Ocean. Although much was uncertain about our future, this trip was in the books. We would treasure what for both of us had been a trip of a lifetime, a lifetime that, in fact, would be molded in some ways due to our journey. We turned and walked our bikes back, heading west for the first time in 4,000 miles, to home and life awaiting us. We would have more adventures, no doubt, and although this was an ending, it was also a beginning.

Epilogue

LEAVING OWLS HEAD *behind, Denise and I continued up the coast of Maine until we once again were in Canada and now headed for Nova Scotia. With a fresh tailwind and a rising sun warming my bones, I looked over at Denise and saw a look of contentment that surely matched my own. With an early start, Denise and I had snuck out of Louis and Vera's home, hoping that they and my father would understand that the tug on us to continue our adventure was too strong to resist. We had no money and our gear was in tough shape, but we had persevered before and were certain we would find a way to continue.*

OK, so that was just a daydream, but it could have easily been reality.

MANY YEARS HAVE now come and gone since that June day in 1981 when Denise and I started our adventure. At the time, we were in our mid-20s, with a dream and the drive and optimism to pursue it. So many times back then, we found ourselves explaining to people why we were even doing this trip. We often worked hard at answers that were intended to convince others that we were doing the right thing. And we had to reassure ourselves from time to time because this trip certainly deviated from the normal route people choose through life. Seldom can we expect rewards if we aren't willing to assume some risk.

Time and again, we encountered people along the way who told us how they wished they would have or could do a trip like we had done. Perhaps more than anything, I think we were pushed by a little bit of fear—of the commitments and responsibilities of new careers and lifestyles that would demand much of our time and energy. Maybe we were also pushed by people deep into their own lives who had encouraged us to "do this now when you can."

Life after our trip did grab hold of us, and we would have struggled to find time to chase dreams in the years that followed. When Denise and I had begun our trip, we had only met ten months earlier. Although we were more than just friends at that point, we hadn't yet committed to anything more serious. A little over a year from the end of our trip, however, we married. In 2012, we celebrated our 30th anniversary with our 28-year-old son Ben and his bride of two years, Lauren.

In 1981, we grabbed tightly onto our dream at a time when we often could only afford to dream. We weren't well off, didn't have the best gear, and had no guarantees we could pull it off. What we did have was good health, the eternal optimism of youth, and a desire burning in each of us to find a way to have a life both rewarding in careers and adventure.

Both of us continued on to become teachers. We have lived the life we had dreamed of in 1981. Having retired this past July, we once again have time to dream about and take extended trips.

As an educator, I've had the opportunity to share stories of our trip with many students over the years, and I had hoped to encourage them to also follow their dreams. I tried to explain the need to find balance in life relative to the old saying, "All work and no play," and so on, as well as its inverse.

While Denise and I built our lives over the past decades, our adventures were small-scale yet ambitious, revolving around active lifestyles of running, skiing, kayaking, and—of course—biking, as well as other activities.

We confronted the challenges of family life, careers, and loss of close friends and family, and of surviving serious health issues. My bout with cancer had taught me so many things; most importantly, to not sweat the small stuff, but instead to pour my heart into the big stuff, and to live every moment of every day. Although I would have chosen to avoid some of these battles, these struggles made the good times that much sweeter.

I could draw so many parallels of our trip to everyday life. Just as our slog through the mud and rain to crest the mountain of the Hope Slide in British Columbia stretched us to our limits, so too, did the headwinds of stress and strain of life sometimes. We often wondered if we'd make it through.

But just like we rolled 30 miles downhill into sunshine once past the Hope Slide that day, we also caught our share of tailwinds through so many of life's challenges.

Today, Denise and I have it darn good. We're still pretty healthy, even though we both carry the creaks and cracks of an active lifestyle that we prefer to view as badges of honor. We're certainly not rich in the minds of many, but if measured by our lifestyle and memories, I would tell you I've enjoyed great wealth. Life, as I suspected, has been like our bike trip. We've had our rainy days but we've been blessed with more sunshine, and just like on the road, it's truly been about the journey.

Today, we are able to carry a credit card on our adventures, stay in motels when we choose to do so, and order as much as we want in restaurants if we're so inclined. Though we travel with a little more comfort, I would not trade anything for that day in June 1981, when we rolled across the Arthur Laing Bridge at the start of our journey with no credit cards or cell phones to save us, $475.00 between us, and 4,000 miles ahead of us.

ON JULY 22, 2012, shortly before this book went to print, a blistering hot, steamy morning dawned on Sioux Center, Iowa, for the 40th RAGBRAI (the Register's Annual Great Bike Ride Across Iowa). The beckoning sunrise welcomed Denise and me along with over 10,000 other riders for this annual pilgrimage across the state. We had first signed up for this ride in 1984 but shortly thereafter we found out that our family would be growing by one (son Ben) and our plans were put on hold. Twenty-eight years later we embarked on this weeklong odyssey under daytime temperatures in excess of 105° Fahrenheit. Fueled by every version of edible pork known to man, as well as countless treats of watermelon and homemade pie, we once again journeyed eastward by bike.

Riding with Team Livestrong, Lance Armstrong's cancer foundation, our team raised over $225,000.00 for the cause. Our team was comprised of cancer survivors and close friends and family members of survivors. Once again I was inspired and this time I was able to give something back.

TIME PASSES FAR too fast, and those days of 1981 seem like yesterday in many ways. My father passed on in 1999, but his influence on me to seek adventures burns as bright as ever. I often catch myself wishing it possible to relive those days, but we all know they are now relegated to memories that can never really be recaptured. Writing this book is perhaps as close as I can come to it, and I realize now as I wrap it up that telling this story has been a journey in and of itself, complete with headwinds and tailwinds. Similarly, just like those days of 1981, this year of writing has been about the journey, and now that the destination is near, I once again find myself not really wanting to stop.

My last journal entry of the trip read, "Life is a gift that is up to us to unwrap." I feel like we had tilled fertile ground on this adventure, planting seeds for future journeys. A new crop of opportunities and dreams will always push its way to the surface, but like seedlings, these dreams would need to be nurtured and tended if we expect them to ripen and produce fruit. And like an old bike that has been well oiled and kept ready to roll, I also am still ready to harvest those opportunities, dreams, and gifts.

What's important now is to chase new dreams. Right now, I feel a tailwind coming up behind me, and it's time to look down the road and ride the breeze.